How To Parent A Child With Eating Disorder(anorexia)

Understanding and Supporting Your Child's Recovery- A Complete Guide

Jennifer M. Stevens

Copyright

All rights reserved. © 2024 Jennifer M. Stevens. Except for brief quotations included in critical reviews and certain other noncommercial uses allowed by copyright law, no part of this book may be reproduced, distributed, or transmitted in any form or by any means, including photocopying, recording, or other electronic or mechanical methods, without the publisher's prior written permission.

Disclaimer⚠

The content of this book is intended only for educational and informational purposes. It is not intended to take the place of professional medical advice, diagnosis, or treatment. Never be afraid to seek advice from your doctor or another qualified healthcare provider when you have questions about a medical issue. Never disregard competent medical advice or postpone seeking it because of something you've read in this book. The publisher and author disclaim all liability for any harm or loss resulting from using the information in this book.

treating the eating disorder's psychological, emotional, and physical aspects while individualized treatment plans are created to match the requirements and objectives of each client.

Over the course of her career, Jennifer has worked in a range of clinical, educational, and advocacy settings. She has collaborated with educators, community organizations, lawmakers, and healthcare professionals to advance awareness and support for those who suffer from anorexia nervosa. She is renowned for her devotion to evidence-based treatment, her kind demeanor, and her belief in enabling people to take charge of their own healing.

Along with her professional work, Jennifer is a prolific writer and speaker who shares her knowledge and perspectives on eating disorders, body image, and mental health through talks, publications, and workshops. Her writing is distinguished by its compassion, lucidity, and emphasis on empowerment. It provides helpful advice and support to people with anorexia nervosa, as well as their families, as they navigate the difficulties associated with the condition.

Jennifer's work demonstrates her steadfast commitment to this objective. She is passionate about promoting awareness, connection, and healing within the eating disorder community. Jennifer continues to have a significant influence on the lives of people impacted by anorexia nervosa through her writing, therapeutic work, and advocacy work. She provides individuals and families with direction, support, and hope as they journey toward recovery and wellness.

Table of contents

Introduction: Navigating the Challenges and Finding Hope

Part I: Understanding Your Child's Journey (Anorexia Nervosa)

Chapter 1: Understanding Anorexia Nervosa.................................19

Chapter 2: Recognizing the Signs and Symptoms of Anorexia Nervosa...........33

Chapter 3: Beyond the Eating: Understanding the Emotional Pain Behind Anorexia...45

Part II: Nurturing Nourishment

Chapter 4: Creating a Supportive Environment at Home........................61

Chapter 5: The Role of Nutrition in Recovery...71
Chapter 6: Meal Planning and Management Strategies.......................89

Part III: Parenting Strategies for Support and Communication

Chapter 7: Communication and Connection: Building Trust and Open Dialogue...................................107
Chapter 8: Setting Boundaries and Providing Structure..127
Chapter 9: Coping with Challenges and Relapses..145

Part IV: Supporting Your Child on the Path to Recovery

Chapter 10: Understanding the Treatment Process...167
Chapter 11: Therapy and Counseling Approaches..187

Chapter 12: Self-Care for Parents and caregiver: Maintaining Your Well-being..203

Part V: Finding Help and Resources

Chapter 13: Finding the Right Treatment Team- Professional Support Services for Families...217

Chapter 14: Educational and Non-Profit Organizations....................................233

Chapter 15: Nourishing Hope Together: A Journey of Recovery.........................249

Appendix: Resources and References

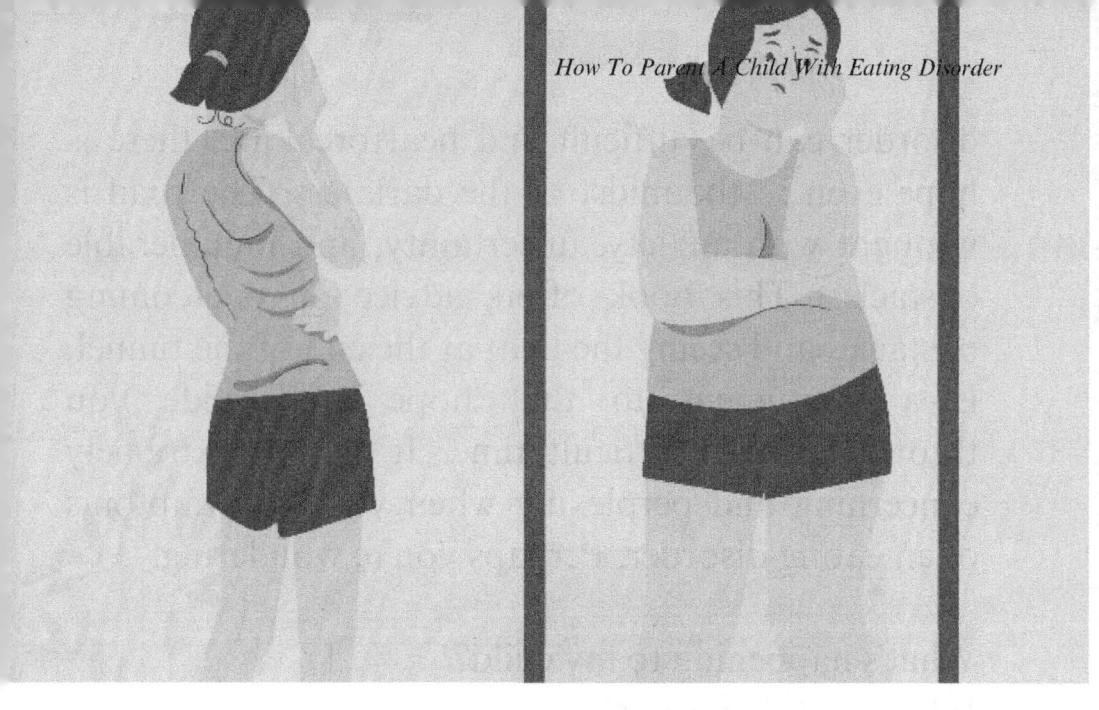

Introduction

Navigating the Challenges and Finding Hope

Welcome to "How To Parent A Child With Eating Disorder(anorexia): Understanding and Supporting Your Child's Recovery- A Complete Guide". For parents and other caregivers starting the journey to help their children navigate the challenges of anorexia nervosa, this book is a beacon of hope. It is your natural instinct as a parent to protect and nurture your child. The experience of raising a child with an eating disorder can be difficult and heartbreaking, there is hope even in the midst of the darkness. The road is wrought with anxiety, uncertainty, and innumerable obstacles. This book offers advice on overcoming obstacles and seeing the light at the end of the tunnel, is a monument to that hope and guide you throughout this difficult time. It can be extremely concerning and perplexing when you see symptoms of an eating disorder. Perhaps you're wondering:

What's happening to my child?
What did I do wrong?
How can I help them get better?

How to parent a child with eating disorder is here to be your companion on this journey. It will provide you the information and encouragement you need to comprehend eating disorders, mainly anorexia nervosa, and navigate the path to recovery for your child.

Anorexia nervosa is not just about diet, it's also about deep-seated fears, emotional distress, and a frantic attempt to gain control. In order to effectively assist and nurture the route to recovery, it is imperative to comprehend the underlying emotional anguish. We shall explore the intricacies of anorexia nervosa in these pages, revealing all of its facets and equipping parents with the information and resources they require to help their kids.

This book will also examine the symptoms and signs of anorexia nervosa. We'll explore the emotional experiences that are occasionally linked to this illness. You'll discover how to establish an environment of safety and support at home, foster open communication with your child, and collaborate efficiently with medical specialists.

Recall that you are not alone at all. Similar difficulties are experienced by many families, and hope is very high. Your child can heal and lead a happy, healthy life with the correct help and direction. Numerous networks of support and services are available to you, such as non-profit and educational institutions that support families impacted by eating disorders. There is support available, and you are not alone.

Who is this book for?

This book is intended for parents and other caregivers who may be worried that their kid or teenager has an eating disorder, especially anorexia nervosa. It is also a valuable resource for anyone who wishes to understand more about eating disorders and how to help people who are impacted by them should definitely check it out.

What this book will cover

This book will provide you with knowledge and support to navigate your child's journey with anorexia nervosa. Here are some key areas it will cover:

Understanding eating disorders anorexia nervosa
Recognizing the signs and symptoms
Exploring the emotional aspects of eating disorders
Creating a supportive home environment
Effective communication strategies
Finding the right treatment team and navigating treatment options
Self-care for parents and caregivers

This book stresses how crucial it is to have your child receive professional assistance from licensed nutritionists, licensed therapists, and doctors at every stage of their recovery.

This book serves as an introduction. It will provide you with information and resources, but it's crucial to keep in mind that it can't take the place of expert assistance. We'll stress how crucial it is that your child receive treatment from licensed physicians, registered nutritionists, and skilled therapists during their recuperation.

We can foster hope for a better future for your child and your family by working together, armed with knowledge, empathy, and a dedication to wellbeing. As we set out on this journey, let's not forget that recovery is achievable. Although there may be a long and difficult road ahead, we can nurture hope and lead our children toward a better, healthier future if we have the patience, understanding, and unwavering support of one other. Let's go off on this path of recovery and restoration together.

Part I

Understanding Your Child's Journey (Anorexia Nervosa)

Chapter 1

Understanding Anorexia Nervosa

Millions of people worldwide suffer from anorexia nervosa, a complicated and sometimes misdiagnosed eating illness that mostly affects teenagers and young adults. Anorexia nervosa resembles self-starvation. Young people with this health issue have a skewed perception of their bodies. They believe they are overweight. They consequently significantly limit their food intake. Additionally, it triggers different behaviors that prevent people from acquiring weight. Children typically consume less than adults do, which frequently includes items that are heavy in fat and carbs.

Teenagers and kids with anorexia want to maintain as low a weight as they can. They may use laxatives, induce vomiting, overexercise, undereat, or any combination of these to achieve this, which might make them really sick.

They frequently have a skewed perception of their bodies, believing they are overweight when in fact they are underweight. The majority of cases of anorexia nervosa occur in young women, usually beginning in the mid-teens.

Let's take a quick look at what anorexia nervosa is before delving into the main features of the condition in this chapter, which will include its definition, prevalence, and factors contributing to its causes.

.

Anorexia, also known as anorexia nervosa, is a severe eating condition that can harm a person's mental and physical well-being. Even in cases where an individual is underweight, it is distinguished by a strong dread of gaining weight. This dread causes unsafe and harmful eating patterns and behaviors.

Here's a breakdown of some key aspects of anorexia nervosa:

Restricted eating: Individuals who struggle with anorexia may drastically cut back on their food intake or completely avoid certain foods. They might eat very little at meals, skip meals, or come up with reasons not to eat.

Distorted perception of one's body: They frequently have a distorted perception of their bodies. Even if they are underweight, they could think of themselves as overweight. Feelings of worthlessness and shame can result from this, which can be quite upsetting.

Obsession with weight: Those with this disorder are obsessed with their body's dimensions and weight. To cover up what they think are imperfections, they might wear baggy clothes, weigh themselves constantly, and become fixated on calories.

Control: If a person is feeling worried or overwhelmed, anorexia may be a method for them to feel in control of something in their life. Limiting one's food intake or engaging in excessive exercise might give one a feeling of control and accomplishment.

It's critical to realize that anorexia nervosa is neither a phase or a way of life. It's a severe mental disorder that has to be treated by a specialist.

Fundamentally, anorexia nervosa is defined by a severe restriction in food intake caused by a skewed sense of one's body and an excessive dread of gaining weight. Anorexics often believe that their activities are necessary to achieve an idealized body form or size, despite the negative physical effects, such as severe weight loss and malnourishment.

Studies on the prevalence of anorexia nervosa have revealed that women and girls account for about 90% of cases that are diagnosed, with a disproportionate impact on this population. But it's important to understand that men and people of all gender identities can also experience difficulties related to this illness. Furthermore, anorexia nervosa affects everyone, regardless of the circumstances; it does not discriminate based on age, social level, or cultural background. It's critical to realize that you are not to blame for acquiring anorexia nervosa and that your attention should be directed toward getting therapy for your child rather than placing blame on yourself. Unresolved negative emotions and past traumas resulting from the intricate intertwining relationships between social, biological, and psychological factors, which can have their roots deep within an individual since early childhood, are sometimes the true causes of anorexia nervosa, rarely having anything to do with food or weight.

Sociocultural, psychological, and biological variables all influence how susceptible a person is to the illness. Anorexia nervosa can develop and worsen due to a variety of factors, including genetic predisposition, neurobiological variations, personality features, and environmental factors such as social pressure to be thin and flawless.

Factors Contributing to The Development of Anorexia Nervosa

Biological factors: Studies indicate that a person's genetic makeup may be a major risk factor for anorexia nervosa. Research has shown that those with a family history of eating disorders are more likely susceptible to the condition, suggesting a possible genetic predisposition. Furthermore, anorexia nervosa may occur as a result of neurobiological variations, including changes in brain chemistry and function. For instance, individuals with the disease have been shown to have anomalies in neurotransmitters such as norepinephrine, serotonin, and dopamine, which may have an impact on reward processing, hunger, and mood control.

Psychological factors: Obsessive-compulsive disorder (OCD), depression, and anxiety disorders are among the mental health illnesses that anorexia nervosa frequently co-occurs with. Restrictive eating habits are a common coping mechanism used by people with anorexia nervosa to deal with trauma, stress, or intense emotions. Perfectionism, low self-esteem, and a strong need for control are some psychological characteristics that are frequently seen in people with the illness. These elements may play a role in the onset and maintenance of anorexia nervosa because people may use food restriction as a way to feel in control of their life and fulfill goals.

Trauma: Trauma can take many different forms, such as witnessing a violent attack, natural disasters, or war, as well as sexual abuse, physical assault, or harsh discipline during infancy. Battle wounds that are verbal, physical, or emotional can cause trauma. Perhaps you were in an abusive love relationship or received harsh discipline on a regular basis as a child. Or perhaps you experienced bullying at school and were constantly contrasted with your siblings as a child? If the unresolved emotions from the traumatic event are not properly addressed, those who have suffered trauma in any form are more likely to develop an eating disorder.

Sociocultural factors: Anorexia nervosa can develop as a result of societal pressure to achieve thinness and adhere to idealized beauty standards. This is especially true for teens and young adults. Unrealistic body ideals can be internalized as a result of widespread diet culture that encourages weight reduction and body dissatisfaction as well as media depictions of thinness as the pinnacle of beauty. Anorexia nervosa risk may also be increased by cultural norms and beliefs surrounding food, weight, and body image, especially in societies where being thin is associated with success, or social acceptance.

It's important to understand that a complex interaction of biological, psychological, and societal factors rather than a single cause contributes to the development of anorexia nervosa. With a greater awareness of these variables, parents and other caregivers may support their children more effectively by addressing the underlying causes of the condition and provide comprehensive treatment that attends to the emotional and physical components of anorexia nervosa.

Parents and other caregivers who are providing support to a child or teen who is battling anorexia nervosa must comprehend the intricacies of the condition. It is a serious mental health illness that calls for compassion, empathy, and all-encompassing treatment; it is not just a matter of willpower or vanity.

Understanding Emotional Anorexia

An extreme fear of gaining weight and an unwillingness to maintain a healthy or average body weight are the hallmarks of anorexia nervosa, a mental disorder. Teenagers and kids with anorexia drastically restrict their food intake; some even use laxatives and diuretics in an attempt to induce vomiting and lose weight.

The majority of individuals are aware of the term anorexia. They associate the phrase with eating disorders, but individuals may also have emotional anorexia. Emotional anorexia, in my opinion, is the inability to experience and process any kind of emotion, from "normal" everyday feelings to "major" or crisis emotions.

The majority of the time, emotional anorexia begins in childhood and worsens with maturity. It acts as a protective mechanism to assist a youngster in coping with difficult, unpleasant, and traumatic situations. Every youngster handles challenging situations differently as they get older. Some kids "turn off" their feelings. Eventually, they come to the realization that it is easier to stop feeling than to carry on experiencing unpleasant feelings. At times, this process proceeds more slowly and subliminally, and some individuals can even recall the precise moment when they chose to suppress their emotions. It is possible to stop feeling pain by turning it off and not caring, but doing so has drawbacks.

During challenging times in your life, you might not have to experience suffering or

grief, but you also lose out on experiencing positive feelings. Our brains are not designed in a way that allows us to simply switch off bad emotions and ignore others. Try not to experience every feeling when you're trying to turn them off. Even in the most momentous of events, you lose out on happiness and delight. Not being able to properly connect with your loved ones is another unpleasant effect. It is impossible to be fully connected to someone if you are not in touch with your innermost thoughts and emotions. Your friends and family will sense it! (As a parent, you might be experiencing this right now.) You won't experience this at first, but it will get harder and more painful as time goes on.
What kind of circumstances, then, might make a child block off their emotions?

Assume, there is a middle school girl named Sarah. She holds herself to an extremely high level and has always been a perfectionist. She has always believed that everything about her, including her appearance and grades must be flawless. But eventually, the strain to be flawless begins to overtake her. She begins to believe that she falls short of her own expectations. She eventually begins to believe that she is powerless over her life. She starts limiting her food consumption in an attempt to take back control of her life. Her restriction causes serious weight loss and other health issues over time.

This is simply one illustration of how emotional variables might play a role in the emergence of anorexia nervosa. The emergence of anorexia nervosa can result from a variety of circumstances.

Children's brains are not developed enough to handle stress or unpleasant circumstances. As a protection strategy to help us survive maturity, we learn to turn off our emotions. The problem is that the defense system does not magically disappear with aging. It's nice when we're kids, but as we become older it usually ruins our relationships.

You have covered the basics of anorexia nervosa in this chapter. You will explore anorexia nervosa many facets in the ensuing chapters, covering its indications and symptoms, the psychological distress that underlies the condition, and useful methods for helping your child recover. By learning more about anorexia nervosa, you may better equip yourselves to provide your kids the loving attention and encouragement they require to overcome this difficult illness.

Chapter 2

Recognizing the Signs and Symptoms of Anorexia Nervosa

Anorexia nervosa (anorexia) can be difficult to identify because people with this condition often go to great lengths to hide their behaviors. Early intervention and therapy for anorexia nervosa depend on the ability to recognize its signs and symptoms. We will examine the different behavioral, emotional, and physical markers of the disorder to provide parents and other caregivers with the information they need to see possible warning signals in their kids.

Notable signs and symptoms of Anorexia

Modifications to Eating Behavior: Missing meals or consuming tiny amounts, Finding reasons not to eat, Establishing strict dietary guidelines or eating customs, Eliminating whole food groupings, unhealthy eating obsession that appears out of control frequent remarks on calories, weight, or food.

Case scenario

Sarah started to eat very little and skip meals. She also developed strict rules about what she could and could not eat, as well as reasons not to eat. She developed an obsession with eating healthily and was always talking about food, weight, and calories.

Physical signs: Notable changes in physical appearance and health are frequently observed as a result of anorexia nervosa. These can include weariness, weakness, dizziness, fainting, and considerable weight loss or being underweight for one's age and height. In an attempt to retain heat, the body may generate a fine covering of hair called lanugo across the body, dry skin, brittle nails, and hair loss or thinning. Low blood pressure, thirst, edema in the arms or legs, tooth erosion and knuckle calluses from vomiting, lack of menstruation, constipation, and pain in the abdomen, dry or yellowish skin, an intolerance for colds, and irregular heartbeats.

> **Case scenario**
> Sheila, a sixteen-year-old high school student, has always participated in athletics. Her relatives and acquaintances have remarked that she appears worn out and reclusive lately. She started thinking up reasons not to eat because she had dropped a lot of weight. Despite her apparent thinness, Sheila seems fixated on her weight and talks about calories all the time.

Beyond only physical symptoms, anorexia can present in other ways as well. A variety of emotional and behavioral changes are common in anorexics. Here are a few more signs to watch out for:

Behavioral signs: People who suffer from anorexia nervosa may display a variety of behaviors pertaining to their eating patterns and self-perception. Extreme dietary restriction, avoiding particular foods or food groups that are thought to be "unhealthy" or "fattening," compulsive calorie monitoring or tracking, and mealtime rituals like chopping food into tiny bits or rearranging it on the plate are a few examples of these behaviors. Excessive exercise is another way that people with anorexia nervosa may try to burn calories and manage their weight. Other behavioral indicators include lying about the amount of food consumed, measuring or weighing the body repeatedly out of fear of gaining weight, constantly examining oneself in the mirror to find perceived flaws, complaining about being overweight or having fat areas of the body, and hiding under layers of clothing.

Emotional signs: Psychological symptoms and severe emotional anguish are frequently present in individuals with anorexia nervosa. Even when severely underweight, people may have a strong dread of gaining weight or becoming "fat." Additionally, they might show increased anxiety in relation to food, eating in public, or food-related social situations. Irritability, mood swings, social disengagement, and an obsession with weight, form, and body image are some additional emotional indicators.

> **Case Scenario**
> Nora has also dropped a significant amount of weight, which worries her parents. They've seen that she appears tense all the time and gets angry fast. She answers their questions about her day in a curt and condescending manner. They used to be open between Nora and them, but lately, there's a wall.

Cognitive signs: Distorted thought patterns about food, weight, and body image are common in anorexia nervosa. People may have a distorted view of the size and shape of their bodies, believing that they are overweight or ugly while in fact they are significantly underweight. Extreme fear and avoidance of weight gain can be exacerbated by this skewed body image, which can result in inflexible and restrictive eating habits. Black-and-white thinking is another behavior that anorexics may exhibit. They may perceive foods as either "good" or "bad" and label themselves as "successful" or "failures" depending on how well they are able to follow tight dietary guidelines.

> **Case Scenario**
> Sarah, a 16-year-old high school student, has always worked diligently and conscientiously, aiming for excellence in whatever she does. But her parents have seen worrying changes in her mood and conduct lately. Sarah has started to withdraw more and more, spending more time by herself in her room and avoiding getting out and about with her friends and family.
> When her parents watch Sarah more closely, they see that she has also developed a severe obsession with her weight and beauty. Despite being notably underweight, she constantly criticizes herself for being "too fat" or "not good enough." Sarah

> has started adhering to stringent dietary guidelines, eliminating whole food groups and carefully tracking her calorie intake at every meal. She cites emotions of shame and guilt over eating as the reason she won't eat in front of other people. Sarah's skewed perception of her body endures in spite of her parents' affirmations that she is healthy and attractive as she is. She stays away from scales and mirrors out of concern that they will make her feel "fat" or "unattractive." Sarah's once-bright and vivacious personality has been eclipsed by melancholy and worry as she battles to keep control over her appearance and eating patterns.

Sarah's case study demonstrates the cognitive symptoms of anorexia nervosa, such as her tight dietary habits, obsession with appearance, and distorted body image. Sarah's self-perception as overweight endures despite her physical fragility and malnourishment, pushing her to drastic steps to regulate her food intake and body size. It is imperative that Sarah's parents identify these cognitive indicators so they may act quickly to support her on her road to recovery and see a specialist.

Social signs: Anorexia nervosa can have a significant impact on a person's relationships, social interactions, and engagement in day-to-day activities. People with the disorder frequently experience social retreat and isolation because they may feel self-conscious or ashamed of their eating habits or appearance. Additionally, because of exhaustion, malnutrition, or obsession with food and weight, people with anorexia nervosa may find it difficult to focus or participate in activities, which can negatively affect their performance at school or at work. Anorexics may also experience anxiety and distress from social activities or food-related gatherings, which makes them avoid these settings completely.

> **Case Scenario**
> David, a 17-year-old, just signed up for the cross-country squad. He's started focusing more on working out and running. David eats relatively little and stays away from meal-related social events. He frequently examines himself in the mirror and appears to be obsessed with his physical image. If David can't work out or thinks he's eaten too much, he gets nervous and agitated.

Parents and siblings may feel confused, frustrated, and helpless in response to their loved one's condition, anorexia nervosa can have a substantial impact on family dynamics and relationships. There may be pressure on family members to step in and fix the issue, which could cause friction and conflict in the home. Parents may also feel guilty or blame themselves for their child's anorexia nervosa development, questioning their own involvement in the illness. It's crucial for families to speak honestly and supportively, seeking professional aid and guidance are required to face the challenges of the condition together.

Parents and other caregivers can better appreciate the complexity of anorexia nervosa and assist their child with compassion if they are aware of the cognitive, social, and family indications of the condition. In order to encourage recovery and restore health and well-being, early intervention and therapy are essential. It's crucial to remember that not everyone who has anorexia nervosa will exhibit the same symptoms, and that each person's level of symptom severity may differ. Furthermore, people with the illness may go to considerable efforts to hide their behaviors and symptoms, which makes it difficult for parents and other caregivers to spot the warning indications.

The Importance of Early Intervention

In order to recover from anorexia, early intervention is essential. People with anorexia have a better chance of making a full recovery the sooner they get expert care. Don't wait to get help if you're worried about your child or someone you know. A medical professional or therapist can offer the direction and assistance required to begin the healing process.

Recall that you are not by yourself. There is optimism despite the comparable hardships faced by many families. Anorexics can recover and have a happy, healthy life with the correct care and assistance.

It's critical for parents and other caregivers to follow their gut feelings and to keep an eye out for any changes in their child's behavior, emotional state, or physical well-being. In the event that you believe your child may be suffering from anorexia nervosa, you should get expert assistance right away. Promoting recovery and stopping the disorder's progression require early intervention and therapy.

Chapter 3

Beyond the Eating: Understanding the Emotional Pain Behind Anorexia

Anorexia nervosa (anorexisa) is often much more than just an eating disorder. It can be a complex way of managing challenging feelings and underlying emotional suffering. We'll be looking at the psychological suffering that underlies anorexia nervosa and how it affects people's attitudes, emotions, and actions. Understanding the psychological factors that contribute to the onset and maintenance of anorexia nervosa is crucial for offering empathetic support and assisting patients in their journey toward recovery.

Understanding the Underlying Emotions

Unhealthy eating patterns and behaviors can be developed by anorexics as a coping strategy for trauma, stress, and overwhelming emotions. Restrictive eating practices may be used by people with the condition as a numbing or suppressing mechanism for uncomfortable emotions such trauma, anxiety, despair, low self-esteem, and perfectionism. Controlling their food intake and body size can help them feel less distressed or inadequate for a while.

Anxiety: Concerns about food, gaining weight, and losing control can cause severe anxiety among anorexic individuals. Excessive exercise or dietary restrictions can temporarily boost control and lessen anxiety.

Depression: The root causes of anorexia may include depressive, hopeless, and worthless feelings. These feelings may be dulled by the eating disorder.

Low self-esteem: A distorted body image and negative self-beliefs are common among anorexics. They might use their appearance and weight as a means of self-satisfaction.

Perfectionism: An unwavering pursuit of excellence can be shown in one's appearance, diet, and level of activity. Inadequacy and embarrassment may result if they believe they don't live up to their own lofty expectations.

Trauma: Anorexia may occasionally arise as a coping strategy following a traumatic incident, such as abuse or neglect.

It's critical to keep in mind that every person has a unique emotional experience. Anorexia has no one specific cause, and different people will experience different emotional triggers.

A strong feeling of worthlessness or unworthiness is one of the emotional themes that underlies anorexia nervosa. Some people can think that reaching and maintaining a specific body type or weight determines their worth as a person. They might internalize messages from society that equate being thin with success, beauty, and self-worth, which would motivate them to pursue thinness obsessively and at all costs.

In addition, anorexia nervosa frequently co-occurs with other mental health issues, including depression, obsessive-compulsive disorder (OCD), and anxiety disorders. These coexisting disorders have the potential to worsen distress levels and increase the disorder's complexity. Anorexics, for instance, may find it difficult to participate in daily activities due to their increased anxiety around food, eating in public, and social settings involving food.

Anorexia nervosa may also develop as a result of trauma and unfavorable life circumstances. Disordered eating behaviors can be a manifestation of feelings of helplessness, guilt, and self-blame stemming from childhood abuse, neglect, bullying, or other forms of trauma. Furthermore, the cycle of emotional suffering and disordered eating can be sustained by the reinforcement of maladaptive coping techniques and the compounding effect of societal demands to adhere to unrealistic body ideals.

The internal conflict over identity and self-perception is a major component of the emotional suffering that underlies anorexia nervosa. People may suffer from a severe sense of alienation from their true selves, believing that their physical attributes are the only things that characterize them. People may experience existential distress, feelings of emptiness, and confusion as a result of this separation as they struggle to define their values and identity beyond their outward appearance.

The internalized shame and self-blame that children with anorexia nervosa endure is another facet of the emotional suffering that underlies the condition. People who internalize negative views about themselves and believe that their bodies are imperfect or undeserving of love and acceptance may result from society's widespread emphasis on thinness and beauty. Feelings of inadequacy and self-doubt are sustained, and the cycle of disordered eating behaviors is fueled by this internalized shame, which can be hard to overcome.

Furthermore, unresolved trauma and complicated emotions are frequently managed by anorexia nervosa through maladaptive coping mechanisms. Restrictive eating habits can be used by people as a means of taking charge of their life and avoiding unpleasant feelings or memories. But in the end, this coping technique feeds emotions of worthlessness and self-hatred, thereby continuing the vicious cycle of emotional suffering.

Anorexia nervosa can also affect a person's relationships and social interactions, which exacerbates feelings of loneliness and isolation. People who experience this kind of guilt and secrecy about their disease may isolate themselves from others and refrain from asking friends and relatives for help. For those who suffer from anorexia nervosa, this social isolation can exacerbate feelings of alienation and mental distress.

The Role of Unhealthy Coping Mechanisms

When faced with challenging emotions, individuals with anorexia may resort to unhealthy coping strategies like:

Limiting food intake: You may feel briefly in control and accomplished by skipping meals, eating very little, or avoiding particular foods.

Exercise compulsively: Excessive exercise can be used as a self-punishment strategy, calorie burning technique, or emotional numbness.

Isolation: Refusing to participate in social events can help a person escape circumstances that make them feel ashamed or anxious.

While these actions might provide some respite in the near term, they eventually lead to greater issues down the road. They can impair one's physical well-being, cause social distancing from close relationships, and complicate the resolution of underlying emotional problems.

Anorexia nervosa can also affect a person's relationships and social interactions, which exacerbates feelings of loneliness and isolation. People who experience this kind of guilt and secrecy about their disease may isolate themselves from others and refrain from asking friends and relatives for help. For those who struggle with anorexia nervosa, this social isolation can exacerbate feelings of alienation and mental distress.

The Importance of Addressing Emotional Needs

It is crucial for children's general growth and well-being to attend to their emotional needs. As parents, we have a responsibility to support our kids' emotional development and resilience in addition to meeting their physical needs. The following justifies the need of attending to emotional needs:

Establishing a foundation of security and trust: Meeting a child's emotional needs helps to establish a foundation of security and trust in the parent-child connection. Children get a sense of safety and trust that enables them to explore the world with resilience and confidence when they feel seen, heard, and loved by their parents.

Promoting healthy attachment: Bonding and a healthy attachment between a parent and child are facilitated by attending to a child's emotional needs. Children that have secure attachment feel stable and supported, which helps them build positive relationships with people throughout their lives.

Supporting social and emotional development: Meeting children's emotional needs enables them to acquire critical social and emotional competencies including self-awareness, empathy, and emotional control. Parents can assist their children in navigating complex emotions, managing stress, and forming positive relationships with others by creating a loving and supportive atmosphere.

Encouraging mental health and wellbeing: Disregarding a child's emotional needs can have a lasting effect on their mental and overall wellbeing. According to research, kids who get regular emotional support from their parents are less likely to deal with anxiety, sadness, and other mental health problems as adults. Parents can assist their children in developing the resilience and coping mechanisms required to successfully traverse life's challenges by placing a high priority on their emotional well-being.

Improving parent-child communication: Taking care of emotional needs encourages candid and open dialogue between parents and kids. Parents who actively listen to their kids' ideas, emotions, and worries foster an atmosphere in which kids feel free to express themselves. The parent-child relationship is strengthened by this open communication, which also enables parents to provide their kids the support and direction they require to succeed.

The Power of Empathy and Understanding

For individuals who struggle from anorexia nervosa, or anorexia, can be a highly solitary condition. It's critical to keep in mind that they have support and care from individuals; they are not alone. One of the most crucial things you can do as a parent or caregiver is to approach the circumstance with compassion and understanding.

Giving your child emotional validation by recognizing their feelings and reassuring them that it's acceptable to experience fear, anger, or sadness. Also, Listening without judgment that is making a secure space for them to freely and honestly express themselves by listening to them without passing judgment.

Remember that anorexia is an illness, not a person's identity, so keep your attention on the individual rather than the eating disorder. Although it might be upsetting to witness someone you care about suffer, it's crucial to keep your distance from disagreements or power struggles centered upon food. Make an effort to foster candid communication and trust.

Finding Healthy Outlets for Emotions

People with anorexia may find that therapy is a useful tool for exploring and addressing their underlying emotions. Outside of therapy, there are healthy outlets you may promote as well, though:

Creative expression: Journaling, painting, or playing music can offer a secure setting for expressing feelings in a constructive manner.

Mindfulness practices: Activities that focus on awareness, such as yoga or meditation, can assist people in learning to better understand their emotions and how to control them.

Physical activity: Getting regular exercise might help you feel better and manage stress. But it's crucial to put your attention on things kids like to do and refrain from using exercise as a form of punishment.

Recovery is a journey, not a destination, so keep that in mind. There will be obstacles in the way, but people with anorexia may acquire appropriate coping mechanisms for their feelings and create happy, meaningful lives with perseverance, support, and expert assistance.

Meeting children's emotional needs is critical to their general development and progress. Parents who prioritize emotional well-being first can foster a loving and encouraging atmosphere where kids feel secure, appreciated, and free to realize their full potential. Additionally, it is critical that parents and other caregivers approach the emotional suffering that underlies anorexia nervosa with understanding, respect, and compassion. You may establish a secure and encouraging atmosphere where your child feels heard and accepted by acknowledging and validating their experiences and feelings.

Your child's sense of connection and belonging can be fostered and feelings of guilt and isolation can be lessened by encouraging open communication and giving them the opportunity to express themselves freely. Additionally, by treating the underlying emotional causes of the condition, you may support your child in creating more resilient and healthy coping mechanisms as well as a strong sense of self-worth.

Part II

Nurturing Nourishment

Chapter 4

Creating a Supportive Environment at Home

For a child who has anorexia nervosa (anorexia) as well as their loved ones, it can be a difficult situation. Creating a supportive environment at home is vital for fostering the mental and physical well-being of a child with anorexia nervosa. Supportive environments are key to helping kids and teens recover from anorexia. This entails establishing a secure, caring environment where children can experience comfort and support. In order to foster this environment and aid in their children's healing, parents can be extremely important. We will look at doable methods in this chapter for creating a kind and supportive environment that encourages recovery, healing, and resilience.

Practical Tactics to Creating A Supportive Environment

- **Provide a secure and accepting atmosphere:** Regardless of your child's anorexia nervosa challenges, you want to create an atmosphere where they feel valued, safe, and accepted for who they are. Instead of making negative remarks about their looks or eating habits, concentrate on showing them love, empathy, and compassion. Use "I" statements Instead of accusatory language, use "I" statements to express your concerns. For example, "I feel worried when you skip meals" instead of "You're being difficult by not eating."

- **Promote open communication:** Let your child know that you are there to listen to them without passing judgment, and provide opportunities for them to share their ideas, feelings, and worries with you and your other family members. As you actively and intently listen to your child, validate their experiences and feelings and provide guidance and support.
- **Set realistic expectations:** Be cautious to have reasonable expectations for your child's recuperation. Acknowledge that growth can be nonlinear and sluggish, and rejoice in little triumphs along the road. Establish clear and constant guidelines for your child's diet, exercise routine, and course of treatment. Refrain from putting undue pressure on them to "get better" quickly; instead, concentrate on giving them constant support and encouragement.

- **Establish routines and structure:** Giving anorexic children routines and structure can help them feel safe and grounded by giving them predictability and consistency. Establish regular mealtimes and let your kids help plan and prepare meals so they can take responsibility for their own dietary needs.
- **Promote self-care:** Assist your child in practicing self-care techniques that aid in emotional health, stress relief, and relaxation. This could involve doing things like yoga, practicing mindfulness, creating art, or going outside. As a parent, you have an obligation to prioritize your own well-being and set an example of excellent self-care practices. Establish limits and schedule time for your personal health.
- **Seek professional assistance:** Don't be afraid to ask for support and assistance for your family and child from professionals. A multidisciplinary team

for treatment composed of medical specialists, dietitians, and therapists can offer all-encompassing care customized to meet your child's specific needs. To connect with people who can relate to your experiences and provide help and encouragement, think about attending a support group for parents of kids with eating disorders.

- **Encourage body positivity and self-acceptance:** By embracing diversity in body shapes and sizes and demonstrating self-compassion, one can foster a positive body image and self-acceptance. Instead than criticizing your own appearance or that of others, concentrate on praising each person's special talents and attributes.
- **Work closely with your child's treatment team:** To guarantee coordinated and thorough care, work closely with your child's treatment team, which may include therapist, dietitians and medical specialists. Participate actively in therapy

sessions, meal preparation, and other areas of your child's rehabilitation process by keeping yourself updated about their treatment plan. Formulate a well-rounded food plan in consultation with a physician or qualified nutritionist. Share meals as a family whenever you can.

- **Create a supportive** mealtime environment: This will help to make mealtimes pleasant and memorable. Instead of forcing or coercing your child to eat, concentrate on encouraging and praising them for their efforts. To aid your child in healing, provide a range of nutrient-dense foods and let them help plan and prepare meals.
- **Establish boundaries and consequences**: Clearly and consistently define the parameters for your child's behavior during meals and other facets of their recovery process. It's important to be clear about your expectations and the

Penalties for crossing boundaries. You should also promote and encourage good behavior. Set limits with compassion but firmness, and if you find it difficult to be consistent, get help from a professional.

Also be ready to enforce penalties for noncompliance with treatment plans; however, do it in an understanding and compassionate manner.

- **Promote relationships with peers and support systems:** Help your child establish relationships with peers and support systems that can relate to them, understand their experiences, and provide understanding, encouragement, and empathy. To exchange information, advice, and experiences, think about making contact with other parents whose children suffer from eating disorders.

- **Develop resilience and patience:** Overcoming anorexia nervosa necessitates tenacity, resilience, and patience. Remember that development could be gradual and nonlinear, and be ready for obstacles and setbacks along the road. Honor your child's accomplishments, no matter how modest, and keep a positive outlook on their future.

Parents and other caregivers must be patient, compassionate, and dedicated in order to provide a supportive environment at home. You may make your child feel safe, supported, and empowered to start the healing process with hope and resiliency by creating a loving and supportive environment.

Empower Your Child

Giving your child authority over their surroundings is a crucial part of fostering a supportive home. Here's how to go about doing it:

Include your child in the choice of treatment: When your child is old enough, let them participate in treatment choices. They may feel more committed to their rehabilitation as a result of this.

Honor their efforts: No matter how little their healing attempts may be, acknowledge and applaud them.

Prioritize progress over perfection: The process of recovery is not linear. There are going to be obstacles in the path. Pay attention to appreciating accomplishments and growing from setbacks.

Recall that establishing a nurturing home environment is a continuous endeavor. Your strategy might need to change as your child's rehabilitation advances. Be understanding and patient, and together enjoy the journey.

As your child navigates the difficulties of anorexia nervosa and works towards recovery, you may further improve their sense of safety, stability, and support by implementing these strategies into your approach to building a supportive atmosphere at home. To ensure that you can continue to give your child the best care possible, remember to put your own needs as a parent first and seek out professional and social help when necessary.

Chapter 5

The Role of Nutrition in Recovery

Nutrition plays a crucial role in the recovery process for kids and teens with anorexia nervosa. The physical health of an individual might be negatively impacted by anorexia nervosa. A healthy diet is crucial for healing and the Importance of Nutrition is essential for healing. The foundation of anorexia recovery is correct nutrition, which gives the body the vital nutrients it needs to mend, heal, and operate. Regaining a healthy weight, increasing energy, bolstering the immune system, controlling mood and sleep cycles, and promoting general wellbeing are all benefits of a proper diet.

One type of qualified healthcare practitioner with a focus on nutrition is a registered dietitian (RD). They can be quite helpful in creating a customized meal plan that suits your child's requirements and tastes.

What a registered dietician can do is:

- Evaluate the dietary requirements of your child
- Make a meal plan that is balanced and incorporates all the dietary groups.
- Adjust any nutritional deficits
- Help your kid increase their calorie intake gradually
- Offer continuous assistance and direction
- General Guidelines for Healthy Eating

Let's examine how crucial diet is for maintaining physical health, fostering mental stability, and speeding up the healing process.

- **Restoring nutritional balance:** Addressing the physical effects of malnutrition and restoring nutritional balance are two of the main objectives of nutrition in the treatment of anorexia nervosa. Deficits in important nutrients, including vitamins, minerals, and macronutrients (fat, protein, and carbs), are common in anorexics. Restoring these nutrients and promoting general health and well-being require a varied and balanced diet.

- **Creating regular eating patterns:** Stabilizing blood sugar levels, controlling metabolism, and encouraging a positive relationship with food all depend on creating regular eating schedules. Encourage your kid to eat at regular intervals during the day, with an emphasis on well-balanced meals that feature a range of foods from all food categories that are high in nutrients. Restrictive eating practices, such as skipping meals, can worsen nutritional inadequacies and feed the cycle of disordered eating.

- **Rebuilding trust with food:** Rebuilding trust with food is a crucial part of the recovery process for people struggling with anorexia nervosa. Encourage your child to explore new foods and flavors fearlessly and with an open mind, curiosity, and adaptability. At mealtimes, create a friendly and nonjudgmental atmosphere while praising and encouraging them for their attempts to try new foods and break bad eating patterns.

- **Dealing with anxiety and worries connected to food:** A lot of people who have anorexia nervosa have severe anxiety and fears related to food, eating in public, and social settings involving food. It's critical to acknowledge your child's emotions and worries and to offer them the kind support and encouragement they need to progressively face and overcome their anxieties. To create customized plans for managing anxiety related to food, think about consulting a licensed dietitian or therapist with expertise treating eating disorders.

- **Monitoring physical health and progress:** It's critical to keep a close eye on your child's physical well-being and nutritional condition to make sure they're getting enough food and support while they recuperate. Maintain regular tabs on your child's weight, vital signs, test results, and other nutritional status markers by working closely with your child's treatment team, which may include a registered dietitian and medical specialists. As your child's requirements and development change, make necessary adjustments to meal plans and nutritional treatments.

- Encourage your child to embrace intuitive eating practices and a good body image. These practices center on paying attention to and respecting your body's signals of hunger and fullness. Instead of relying on external rules or limits, teach your child to trust their body's cues and treat them with kindness and respect. Create a welcoming and body-positive atmosphere in your house by highlighting the individual talents and attributes of every person, regardless of their size or shape.

- **Addressing nutritional deficiencies:** Because of their restrictive eating habits and malnourishment, anorexics frequently suffer from severe nutritional deficiencies. Deficits in these areas can have detrimental effects on one's physical well-being and may be a contributing factor in conditions like electrolyte imbalances, bone loss, and cardiovascular problems. Working closely with a licensed dietitian or nutritionist is crucial in order to pinpoint these deficiencies and treat them with specific dietary modifications and, if required, supplements.

- **Handling refeeding syndrome:** In people with anorexia nervosa, refeeding syndrome is a potentially fatal complication that can arise in the early phases of nutritional therapy. It is typified by changes in fluid balance, electrolyte imbalances, and metabolic disruptions that can result in major health issues such cardiac arrhythmias, respiratory failure, and neurological symptoms. Nutritional rehabilitation should be started gradually and properly supervised by medical personnel, paying special attention to electrolyte balance and fluid status, in order to reduce the danger of refeeding syndrome.

- **Supporting gastrointestinal health:** Because of their restrictive eating patterns and malnourishment, anorexics may have gastrointestinal symptoms such bloating, constipation, and problems with gastrointestinal motility. A key component of nutritional rehabilitation is supporting gastrointestinal health, and dietary therapies should emphasize encouraging regular bowel movements, maximizing nutrient absorption and digestion, and reducing discomfort and digestive distress.

- **Incorporating flexibility and variety:** To encourage enjoyment and satisfaction, encourage your child to approach nutrition with flexibility and openness by introducing them to a wide range of foods and flavors. To promote a sense of empowerment and autonomy, encourage kids to try new foods and recipes and engage them in meal planning and preparation. Instead of enforcing strict food guidelines, emphasize the value of moderation and balance, and help your child choose a nutritional pattern that they find satisfying and enduring.

- **Taking care of co-occurring medical issues:** People with anorexia nervosa may also have other medical conditions that call for careful nutritional treatment. For example, nutritional measures like getting enough calcium and vitamin D may help people with osteoporosis maintain healthy bones. In a similar vein, people with digestive problems could find relief from symptoms like reflux or bloating through dietary changes. In order to address any co-occurring medical disorders and make sure your child's nutritional needs are being addressed, it's critical to collaborate closely with their treatment team.

The physical and mental health of your child as well as their path to anorexia nervosa recovery can be greatly enhanced by incorporating these nutritional ideas into your strategy. Recall to approach nutrition with empathy, adaptability, and patience, keeping in mind that healing is a slow, uneven process that calls for constant assistance and direction.

The importance of family meals and shared mealtimes on the role of nutrition in recovery from anorexia nervosa

Family meals are essential for encouraging positive eating habits, nutritional rehabilitation, and creating ties between family members. During meals together, parents and siblings can set an example of healthy eating habits, encourage acceptance of food, and strengthen positive attitudes about food and body image. In addition, family meals provide a safe, comfortable situation in which people with anorexia nervosa can practice confronting their worries and anxiety related to food in a supportive, nonjudgmental manner.

Establishing a welcoming atmosphere during mealtimes: When organizing family dinners, pay special attention to establishing a welcoming and inclusive atmosphere that promotes involvement and engagement from every family member. At the dinner table, steer the conversation away from dieting, weight, and body size and toward more upbeat, neutral subjects that foster enjoyment and connection. Encourage your child to participate actively in meal planning and preparation, giving them the freedom to voice their preferences and make decisions in a nonjudgmental and encouraging environment.

Creating mealtime customs and rituals: This can help establish a sense of routine and structure around eating, resulting in predictable and pleasurable mealtimes for the family. Think about implementing customs like assembling the table, exchanging highlights and troughs of the day, or expressing thanks for the meal and companionship. By reinforcing the value of connection, thankfulness, and shared experiences, these rituals can help create a happy atmosphere during mealtimes.

Promoting mindful eating strategies: During family meals, teach your kids to eat mindfully by concentrating on appreciating the tastes, textures, and feelings of the food without distraction or judgment. Urge them to eat consciously and slowly, giving themselves enough time to savor and appreciate every bite, as well as to pay attention to signals of hunger and fullness. By encouraging a feeling of pleasure and satisfaction from eating, mindful eating strategies can assist individuals who experience anorexia nervosa in forming a more intuitive and positive relationship with food.

We emphasize the importance of relationships, positive reinforcement, and social support in the recovery process. Family meals offer a priceless chance for those suffering from anorexia nervosa to practice and repeat appropriate eating habits in a caring and supportive setting, fostering mental and physical health and speeding up the healing process.

The following are some broad recommendations for encouraging wholesome eating practices when anorexics are recovering:
-Make an effort to eat a range of nutrient-dense foods: At every meal, include fruits, vegetables, whole grains, lean protein sources, and healthy fats.

-Eat regular meals and snacks: Throughout the day, try to have three meals and two or three snacks. This reduces the chance of overeating and helps control blood sugar levels

-Establish an upbeat environment during meals: During meals, keep the conversation focused and steer clear of distractions like TV or phones.

-Make family mealtimes a priority: Eat meals as a family whenever feasible. This may foster a feeling of solidarity and normalcy.

-Remain calm and don't put pressure on yourself: It takes time to recover. Refrain from pressuring your child to consume more food than they feel ready for.

Recall that these are only suggestions. A qualified RD can design a customized plan to fit your child's unique requirements and preferences.

Supporting a Positive Relationship with Food

Anorexia nervosa (anorexia) often involves a distorted relationship with. Recovering entails not only reestablishing wholesome eating routines but also reestablishing a positive relationship with food. Here are a few strategies to help with this process:

Focus on the sensory aspects of eating: Teach your kids to appreciate the flavor, texture, and aroma of food.

Include your child in food preparation: Let your child help plan and prepare meals when they are old enough. They may feel more invested in the process and in control as a result.

Introduce novel meals gradually: Avoid giving your kids too many strange foods. Introduce new possibilities first, but do so gradually and encouragingly.

Be cautious of the topics you discuss during meals: stay away from topics like calories, weight, or diets at the table. Concentrate on having neutral, upbeat chats.

Building a Positive Food Culture

A child's relationship with food can be severely disrupted by anorexia nervosa. Recovering entails more than just picking up wholesome eating practices; it also entails creating a new, positive connection with food. One strategy to promote a healthy eating culture in the house is to emphasize the enjoyment of food. Food may be a source of joy and shared experiences in addition to being a source of nutrition. Explore various cuisines, collaborate on new culinary creations, and honor the social and cultural significance of food. Encourage your child to pay attention to their body's signals of hunger and fullness by practicing mindful eating yourself. They can cultivate a more intuitive relationship with food by practicing mindful eating. Establish a good example for your child when it comes to eating well, also try to set an example for healthy eating habits. Aim to eat a wide range of nutrient-dense foods and steer clear of discussions about restricted dieting.

Recovery is a journey, so expect some setbacks along the road. Be encouraging, patient, and happy for even the little successes. Please take note that while this chapter offers general information about nutrition, always get individual advice on your child's needs from a physician or registered dietician.

Chapter 6

Meal Planning and Management Strategies

Meal planning and management is essential to promoting anorexia nervosa recovery. Meal preparation in advance helps guarantee that children receive the nourishment they require and relieve some of the stress on them. To help children and teenagers feel more at ease when eating, parents should also implement techniques like family meals, frequent snacks, and flexible meal planning. Children and teenagers can start to heal and change their eating patterns if the proper techniques are put in place.

Working together is essential, and creating a meal plan should be a team effort so as to empower your child and encourage a sense of ownership over their recovery, so always include them in the process (as age-appropriate as possible).

The following general actions to keep in mind are:

-Speak with a medical professional: A physician or registered dietitian can evaluate your child's unique needs and provide a customized food plan that satisfies those needs.

-Pay attention to a balanced diet: Try to incorporate a range of nutrient-dense items from every food group into each meal. This guarantees that the body gets the vital nutrients required for recovery and general health.

-**Make a schedule for meals and snacks:** Plan your day to include three meals and two to three snacks. This lowers blood sugar levels and avoids overeating by preventing intense hunger pangs.

-**Establishing a Helpful mealtime** Ambience: Establish a regular eating plan. Eating meals and snacks at the same time each day helps control the body's hunger signals and fosters a sense of routine.

-**Reduce the number of distractions:** During mealtimes, turn off electronics like TVs and phones. Concentrate on striking up a good conversation and environment.

Mealtimes should be about enjoying food and nourishing the body, not about tracking calories or weight.

Strategies for planning balanced meals, managing mealtime challenges, and fostering a positive mealtime environment

- **Collaborate with a registered dietitian**: Collaborate closely with a registered dietitian with expertise in eating disorders to create a customized meal plan that meets your child's specific dietary requirements and preferences. In addition to meeting your child's nutritional needs, a trained dietitian can offer advice on how to prepare balanced meals that take into account their unique dietary needs and difficulties.

- **Place an emphasis on balanced nutrition:** Pay particular attention to preparing meals that are balanced and comprise a range of nutrient-dense foods from all dietary groups, such as fruits, vegetables, dairy products, and meat and/or protein sources. To support general health and well-being, encourage your child to eat a balanced mix of macronutrients and micronutrients.

- **Incorporate flexibility and diversity:** Provide a large selection of foods and flavors to promote flexibility and variety in meal planning. To help your child develop a sense of empowerment and autonomy, let them try different foods and recipes and get them involved in meal planning and preparation. Instead of enforcing strict food guidelines, emphasize the value of moderation and balance, and help your child choose a nutritional pattern that they find satisfying and enduring.

- **Deal with worries and anxiety about food:** Recognize the worries and fears your child may have around eating, and together, come up with plans for handling and conquering these obstacles. To help your child face and overcome their concerns, gently support and encourage them to approach food with curiosity, openness, and flexibility. To create customized plans for managing anxiety related to food, think about consulting a licensed dietitian or therapist with expertise treating eating disorders.

- **Manage mealtime challenges:** Be ready to deal with difficulties and roadblocks during meals with tolerance and kindness. Establish reasonable expectations for conduct during meals and consistently offer praise and support for healthful eating habits. When it comes to mealtime habits that could be damaging or disruptive, set clear boundaries and consequences. If you find it difficult to handle mealtime challenges effectively, get professional help.

- **Encourage a positive atmosphere at mealtimes:** Establish a welcoming and nonjudgmental atmosphere that encourages unwinding, delighting, and interacting. At the dinner table, steer the conversation away from dieting, weight, and body size and toward more upbeat, neutral subjects that promote enjoyment and connection. Give your child gentle encouragement and praise for trying to overcome concerns and restrictive eating habits, and encourage them to approach meals with interest and openness.

- **Encourage your child to eat mindfully:** At mealtimes, help your child to practice mindful eating by emphasizing being in the present and being aware of their body's signals of hunger and fullness. Slowing down, enjoying every bite, and focusing on the flavor, texture, and aroma of the food are all part of mindful eating. Instruct your youngster to chew slowly, set down their utensils between bites, and take breaks to pay attention to their. bodies' signals of hunger and fullness. In addition to fostering a better relationship with food, mindful eating can help anorexics better understand and react to their bodies' natural hunger and satisfaction signals.

- **Address dietary preferences and restrictions:** When organizing meals, take into account your child's dietary preferences and restrictions. Together, come up with some tasty and nutritious substitutes. To accommodate a range of tastes and preferences, think about combining a variety of textures, flavors, and cooking techniques. To make sure that their preferences are taken into consideration, encourage your child to express their likes and dislikes in an honest manner and involve them in the meal planning process.

- **Prepare for difficult situations:** Be ready for difficult situations that can come up at mealtimes, such as get-togethers with friends, special occasions, or eating out. Develop coping mechanisms and backup plans with your child so that they can handle these circumstances well. Use calming strategies, like deep breathing exercises or visualization, to assist your child in managing their anxiety and discomfort in stressful mealtime scenarios. Encourage your child to express their wants and worries in an honest manner, and when necessary, offer comfort and support.

- **Monitor progress and make necessary adjustments:** Keep an eye on your child's development in meal preparation and management over time, and be ready to modify your strategy in light of their unique requirements and advancement. Monitor their food consumption, eating habits, and emotional reactions to meals. Utilize this data to pinpoint areas that require development and enhancement. Collaborate closely with your child's medical team to track their development and modify their diet plan as necessary to help them continue their healing process.

- **Celebrate accomplishments and milestones:** No matter how tiny, acknowledge your child's accomplishments and milestones in meal preparation and management. Give them credit for their efforts and advancement, and commemorate their successes by offering words of wisdom, support, and encouragement. Encourage your child to keep moving closer to their recovery objectives by using positive reinforcement to support healthy eating habits. As a family, celebrate victories and emphasize the value of cooperation and support in overcoming obstacles and realizing goals.

In order to help your child heal and recover from anorexia nervosa, you can further support their nutritional. needs, encourage healthy eating habits, and establish a loving and supportive mealtime environment. It is important to keep in mind that meal planning and management require flexibility, patience, and compassion. Seek assistance from trained professionals when necessary to guarantee your child receives the customized attention and support they require.

The importance of involving the entire family in meal planning and preparation

Including the whole family in meal preparation and planning can foster a sense of shared accountability, cooperation, and connection through food. Encourage every member of the family to share their favorite recipes, come up with meal ideas, and help with meal preparation by chopping veggies, setting the table, or cooking together. Planning and preparing meals as a family not only divides labor but also encourages a sense of pride and commitment in the mealtime ritual.

Promoting communication and family bonding: Organizing and preparing meals is a great way to foster these qualities. Take advantage of this opportunity to catch up on each other's days, swap tales, and establish casual, easygoing connections. In order to create a loving and caring environment where everyone feels heard, respected, and accepted, family members should be encouraged to communicate openly and honestly with one another and to actively listen to one another.

Promoting independence and teaching life skills: Getting kids and teenagers involved in meal preparation and planning helps impart valuable life skills as well as independence and self-reliance. In the kitchen, encourage your child to take on age-appropriate duties and tasks like measuring ingredients, following directions, and preparing simple dishes. The development of practical cooking skills and self-assurance in the kitchen can help children and adolescents suffering from anorexia nervosa feel more capable and autonomous when it comes to meeting their nutritional needs.

Building positive associations with food and mealtimes: Involving family members in the planning and preparation of meals can contribute to the development of wholesome associations with food and mealtimes, fostering a positive relationship with nourishment and eating. Provide an environment that is encouraging and judgment-free so that kids can try new foods, taste different flavors, and express their preferences without worrying about being judged or criticized. Instead of concentrating only on a food's calorie count or nutritional value, use mealtimes to celebrate food as a source of pleasure, connection, and nourishment.

Planning and preparing meals as a family not only creates a supportive and encouraging environment at mealtimes, but it also helps children and adolescents with anorexia nervosa develop resilience, independence, and critical life skills.

Promoting a Positive Meal Experience

A person's relationship with food can be severely disrupted by anorexia nervosa. Recovery includes creating a positive association with mealtimes in addition to reestablishing healthy eating habits. This can be achieved by Focusing on the sensory qualities of food by teaching your kids to appreciate the taste, feel, and scent of their food. Incorporating social and cultural components, together, try out various culinary traditions. This can broaden your child's perspective on food and make mealtimes more engaging. Also, including your child in meal preparation and planning when it is appropriate for their age encourages a positive feeling of control and ownership over the undertaking.

Sample Meal Schedule

This is a general sample and should not be a substitute for a personalized meal plan created by a doctor or registered dietitian.

Breakfast: Whole-wheat toast with nut butter and fruit, oatmeal with nuts and seeds, yogurt with granola and berries.

Lunch: Sandwich on whole-wheat bread with lean protein and vegetables, salad with grilled chicken or fish, leftovers from dinner.

Dinner: Salmon with roasted vegetables and brown rice, chicken stir-fry with whole-wheat noodles, lentil soup with whole-grain bread.

Snacks: Fruits with nut butter, vegetables with hummus, yogurt with granola, hard-boiled eggs.

For specific advice on developing a meal plan for your child, always consult with a registered dietitian and seek professional guidance. This is crucial for creating a safe and effective meal plan tailored to your child's specific requirements.

Part III

Parenting Strategies for Support and Communication

Chapter 7

Communication and Connection: Building Trust and Open Dialogue

Anorexia nervosa, often known as anorexia, can seriously impair trust and communication within families. A solid and trustworthy bond between parents and their children is fostered by effective communication and connection, which also supports anorexia nervosa recovery.

A brief overview of the importance of building trust and maintaining open communication

By actively listening to your child and paying close attention to what they are saying, both verbally and nonverbally, you may create the safe place your child needs to feel comfortable expressing their thoughts and feelings in an honest and judgment-free manner. Respect their emotions and give credence to what they've experienced. You should try these successful communication techniques.

Ask open-ended questions: Encourage your child to go into more detail about their feelings and ideas rather than just a yes-or-no response.

Remain in the now: Steer clear of ruminating on previous transgressions or being entangled in accusations of fault.

Demonstrate compassion and understanding: Consider things from your child's point of view and recognize the difficulties they are experiencing.

Follow through on commitments: If you make a promise, don't hesitate to carry it through. This establishes your dependability and fosters trust.

Observe boundaries: As vital as it is to communicate openly, you also need to honor your child's right to privacy.

Practical Strategies to build trust, encourage dialogue, and strengthen parent-child bonds amidst anorexia nervosa

- **Create a secure and judgment-free environment:** Building open communication and trust with your child requires creating a safe and judgment-free environment in which they feel comfortable sharing their ideas, emotions, and worries. Instead of scolding or humiliating your child for their anorexia nervosa issues, have understanding, empathy, and compassion-filled chats instead. Reassure your child that you are always available to support them and encourage them to talk honestly about their experiences.

- **Engage in active listening:** Trust-building and open communication with your children depend on your ability to actively listen to them discuss their ideas, feelings, and worries without interjecting or passing judgment. Recognize nonverbal clues as well as spoken ones, and validate your child's experiences and feelings by showing empathy and acknowledging their feelings. To show that you comprehend your child's viewpoint and genuinely care about their well-being, consider back what you have heard.

- **Encourage empathy and understanding:** Developing empathy and understanding for your child's struggles and experiences is crucial to forging a solid and encouraging bond. Place yourself in your child's position and make an effort to understand the world from their point of view, recognizing the challenges they encounter and confirming their emotions and experiences. Instead of downplaying or ignoring your child's difficulties, show them that you care and that they are supported.

- **Promote open and honest communication:** Promote open and honest communication within your family and give your kids the chance to voice their ideas, emotions, and worries without worrying about criticism or retaliation. Encourage your family to have an honest and open culture where everyone is at ease discussing their thoughts and experiences in a polite and open manner. Set an example of open communication by sharing your own thoughts, feelings, and experiences with your child in an open and transparent manner.

- Set aside time each day or each week for open discussion and connection with your child. This time should be free from interruptions and distractions. Take use of this time to visit with your child, talk about any difficulties or worries they may be having, and provide assistance and direction as required. Establish a consistent schedule of transparent dialogue and interaction to help your youngster feel safe and predictable.

- **Validate your child's experiences**: Establishing a sense of connection and understanding as well as establishing trust require you to validate your child's feelings and experiences. Even if you may not quite understand or agree with them, acknowledge your child's battles with anorexia nervosa and respect their feelings and concerns. Remind your child that you are here to help them on their recovery journey and that their experiences are valid.

- **Seek professional assistance when needed**: Don't be afraid to get help from therapists, counselors, or other mental health specialists if you are having trouble connecting with your child or meeting their needs. An experienced specialist can help with anorexia nervosa recovery by providing direction, encouragement, and methods for enhancing parent-child bonding and communication.

- **Creating a Supportive Environment:** Family interactions can be severely impacted by anorexia nervosa, also known as anorexia. Focusing on family activities is one method to create a supportive environment that aids in healing. Spending time together engaging in things that all of you enjoys helps to reinforce family relationships and produce cherished memories; Steer clear of discussions about food or weight at the dinner table: Mealtimes should be spent with family, and friends, not worrying about weight or attractiveness; Communicate truthfully and candidly: Remind your child that you are always available to them and that you value their honest and open communication about their feelings.

The Aspects of Communication and Connection in the Framework of Supporting Recovery

Validate sentiments without reinforcing behavior: It's critical to acknowledge and validate your child's experiences and feelings, but it's also critical to prevent unintentionally encouraging disordered behaviors linked to anorexia nervosa. Promoting recovery requires finding a balance between acknowledging emotions and subtly confronting dysfunctional behaviors. Recognize your child's feelings and challenges with compassion and understanding. At the same time, help them create more positive coping mechanisms by supporting their efforts to question negative beliefs and actions.

Develop empathy and compassion: Developing empathy and compassion for your child's struggles is crucial to creating a solid and encouraging relationship. Instead of passing judgment or offering criticism, try to understand the underlying emotions causing your child's anorexia nervosa problems and behaviors. Reassure your child that you are always there to support them and validate their experiences and feelings, even if you don't entirely understand them.

Promote empowerment and autonomy: Giving your kids the tools they need to actively participate in their own healing can help them feel more empowered, self-sufficient, and autonomous. Your child should be encouraged to take charge of their own recovery, set goals for themselves, and engage in treatment decisions. Give your kids the chance to voice their opinions and make decisions about their care and recuperation so they can feel empowered to take charge of their own rehabilitation.

Encourage the development of resilience and coping mechanisms: Long-term recovery from anorexia nervosa depends on the development of resilience and coping mechanisms. Encourage your child to learn good coping mechanisms, such journaling, mindfulness, relaxation techniques, and engaging in pleasant activities, to help them deal with stress, anxiety, and tough emotions. To assist your child in developing useful coping mechanisms for handling triggers and setbacks, provide an example of resilience and adaptive coping techniques yourself and provide direction and support.

Deal with family dynamics and communication styles: Pay attention to how your child's healing process may be impacted by family dynamics and communication styles. Determine whether your child's anorexia nervosa struggles are a result of any underlying disputes, tensions, or communication patterns, and then work as a family to address and resolve these issues. Encourage your family to have a mutually respectful, understanding, and supportive atmosphere where everyone feels heard, appreciated, and accepted.

Cultivate patience and perseverance: Overcoming anorexia nervosa takes patience, tenacity, and persistence. Be ready for highs and lows throughout the journey, and never waver in your commitment to helping your child get through whatever obstacles they may encounter. Honor minor triumphs and achievements, and provide support and comfort when things go tough. Recall that healing is a gradual process and that your child's journey towards healing and resilience can greatly benefit from your steadfast support and devotion.

You may help your child negotiate the difficulties of recovery with resilience and hope by building a strong and trusting relationship with them, encouraging honest communication and understanding, and offering the support and direction they require. Throughout your child's healing process, keep in mind to prioritize developing a relationship of trust and compassion with them and to approach communication with empathy, compassion, and patience.

The Importance of setting Boundaries and Maintaining Consistency in Communication and Connection in Supporting Recovery from Anorexia

Setting boundaries and maintaining consistency: In the context of assisting anorexics in their recovery, setting clear and consistent boundaries is crucial for fostering a sense of safety, predictability, and trust in the parent-child connection. Establish clear and firm boundaries regarding your child's behavior at meals, their adherence to therapy, and other areas of their recovery process. When setting boundaries, be stern yet kind, and when required, consistently carry out the consequences.

Communicate expectations and consequences: Clearly communicate your expectations for your child's behavior and involvement in their healing process. You should also spell out the repercussions for pushing boundaries or acting in a damaging way. Express your demands and concerns using assertive communication strategies, including "I statements," to avoid placing blame or criticism on others. Encourage your child to accept accountability for their decisions and behaviors, and together you can create plans for handling difficult circumstances.

Prioritize self-care and well-being: As a parent or caregiver, it is crucial to put your own needs and well-being first in addition to helping your kid on their path to recovery. Prioritize activities and practices that support and rejuvenate you, and establish boundaries around your own time, energy, and emotional resources. Seek assistance from loved ones, friends, or organizations that support parents of children with eating disorders. You may also want to think about doing things that you enjoy and find fulfilling outside of your caregiving responsibilities.

Seek professional advice and support: If you are having trouble establishing limits or upholding consistency in your family, don't be afraid to see family therapists or mental health specialists for advice and assistance. A qualified expert can provide advice on how to manage family dynamics, set up appropriate boundaries, and enhance communication in a way that will aid in your child's rehabilitation. Keep in mind that you don't have to go through this path alone and that asking for help is a show of strength.

In order to support anorexia nervosa recovery, it is required to establish boundaries and maintain consistency in your approach to communication and connection. You can establish a loving and caring environment that promotes healing, resilience, and growth for both your child and your family as a whole.

The Significance of Fostering a Sense of Purpose and Meaning

- **Fostering a sense of purpose and meaning:** In order to help your child recover from anorexia nervosa, you should encourage them to develop a sense of meaning and purpose in their lives. Encourage your child to develop meaningful objectives and pursuits that offer them joy and fulfillment by supporting them as they explore their interests, passions, and values. A sense of direction, motivation, and fulfillment beyond their struggles with anorexia nervosa can be given to your child by nurturing a sense of purpose and meaning, whether it be through pursuing academic or career aspirations, taking part in creative hobbies or artistic endeavors, or volunteering or advocating for causes.

- **Promoting self-discovery and personal development:** Overcoming disordered eating behaviors is only one aspect of anorexia nervosa recovery; other goals include regaining one's sense of self, investigating one's identity, and fostering personal growth. Encourage your child to explore their values, beliefs, and goals by supporting them in self-discovery activities like journaling, mindfulness exercises, or self-reflection exercises. Give your kids the chance to discover new passions, interests, and abilities while acknowledging and celebrating their progress toward goals.

- **Resilience and hope-building:** Overcoming the obstacles of anorexia nervosa recovery and fostering optimism and confidence in the future require the cultivation of resilience and hope. Encourage your child to learn resilience-building abilities like stress management, emotion control, and problem-solving, and assist them in coming up with constructive methods to deal with obstacles and disappointments. Encourage your family to have an optimistic and hopeful culture where everyone has faith in your child's ability to overcome challenges and accomplish their goals. Remind them that recovery is achievable with patience, courage, and willpower.

- **Nurturing meaningful connections and relationships:** For those in recovery from anorexia nervosa, building meaningful connections and relationships with others can be quite helpful in terms of support and encouragement. Urge your child to make supportive friends, look for mentors or role models who encourage and motivate them, and fortify their relationships with loved ones and family. Give your kids the chance to participate in community events, social gatherings, or support groups so they can make connections with people who understand, sympathize with, and encourage them based on shared experiences.

With the aim to promote anorexia nervosa recovery, it is crucial to instill a sense of meaning and purpose in your approach to communication and connection. By doing this, you may enable your kid to develop a sense of identity, fulfillment, and purpose that extends beyond their eating disorder challenges. Recovery is a journey, so expect some setbacks along the road. Show tolerance, encouragement, and joy for any accomplishment, no matter how little it may be. Seek out expert assistance, In addition to offering advice on effective communication techniques, a therapist can assist in addressing any underlying emotional issues which might be fueling the eating disorder.

Chapter 8

Setting Boundaries and Providing Structure

Anorexia Nervosa can cause problems with boundary-setting and maintaining stability in families. In order to promote anorexia nervosa recovery and provide a loving and supportive atmosphere for your child, you must establish limits and provide structure. This chapter will discuss the value of structure and boundaries, as well as helpful methods for defining limits that are consistent, encouraging consistency, and building a structured framework that will aid in your child's rehabilitation.

The Importance of Setting Boundaries and Structure

Setting boundaries and providing structure are crucial in helping a child or adolescent navigate the difficult process of recovering from anorexia nervosa. These components are essential for developing a sense of security, encouraging healthy behaviors, and speeding up the healing process in addition to providing a steady and encouraging atmosphere. The following main points emphasize how crucial it is to provide structure and boundaries:

- **Creating Predictability:** In everyday life, predictability is established by boundaries and structure. For those in recovery from anorexia nervosa, predictability is consoling since it lessens uncertainty and anxiety. Emotional health depends on a sense of consistency, which is provided by knowing what to anticipate from mealtimes, therapy sessions, and other events.

- **Fostering Healthy patterns:** Especially when it comes to meals and snacks, structure helps create and preserve healthy patterns. In order to rebuild a positive relationship with food, people with anorexia nervosa must follow regular eating schedules. Regular mealtimes support an individual's overall physical and mental health by normalizing eating habits.
- **Establishing a Safe Space:** Clearly defined boundaries help to establish a safe environment where people feel understood and protected. Reducing the risk of relapse and prioritizing rehabilitation in an environment where detrimental behaviors linked to anorexia nervosa, like restrictive diet and excessive activity, are limited.
- **Supporting Treatment Adherence:** Consistency in treatment regimens is maintained with the help of structure. Adherence to the specified treatment plan

is encouraged by having an organized framework, which may include therapy sessions, medical check-ups, or nutritional advice. Maintaining this consistency is essential for monitoring development and making the required modifications to aid in further healing.
- **Encouraging Accountability:** Boundaries encourage accountability by offering a structure for it for the person as well as their support network. People are motivated to accept accountability for their acts and actively engage in their rehabilitation when expectations and consequences are made apparent. A sense of empowerment and responsibility over the healing process is fostered by this accountability.
- **Reducing Stress Associated with Decision-Making:** People who suffer from anorexia nervosa frequently struggle with making decisions about what to eat, how much to eat, and how to arrange their meals.

Setting up organized meal plans and boundaries might help reduce the stress associated with making decisions.

- **Improving Emotional Regulation:** By offering a framework for handling stresses and triggers, structure helps in emotional regulation. People who follow a regular schedule might build resilience and coping skills to deal with life's obstacles better. Relapse prevention and mental health maintenance depend heavily on this emotional control.
- **Encouraging Independence:** Boundaries should allow for the growth of independence even as they offer structure. People are allowed the freedom to make decisions within reasonable bounds when boundaries are specified. This autonomy promotes self-efficacy and control, two qualities necessary for long-term rehabilitation.

Understanding the significance of Establishing structure and boundaries is a vital part of setting up a setting that aids in anorexia nervosa recovery. It helps the person move toward a healthier, more balanced life by laying the groundwork for accountability, safety, and consistency. A comprehensive strategy that tackles the challenges of eating disorder treatment combines structure with compassion, understanding, and tailored care.

Effective Methods to Set Boundaries, Ensure Consistency, and Create a Supportive Environment for Your Child's Recovery Journey

- **Establish clear and consistent boundaries:** Set limits for your child's behavior during mealtimes, adherence to treatment, and other areas of their recovery process. Be consistent in enforcing these boundaries and communicate them in an assertive and open manner. When someone crosses boundaries or engages in destructive behavior, clearly outline the consequences and carry them out when needed.

- **Promote open communication and cooperation:** Promote family members' cooperation in establishing and upholding boundaries as well as their open communication. Include your child in the process of setting limits and give them the opportunity to voice any feelings, ideas, or concerns they may have about them. Actively listen to what your child has to say, and when necessary, be prepared to compromise and negotiate.

- **Be firm but compassionate:** It's critical to establish and uphold boundaries consistently, but it's also critical to do so with empathy, understanding, and compassion. Instead than using severe punishment or discipline, approach setting boundaries with a supportive and compassionate attitude. Even though you may not agree with your child's actions, validate their feelings and experiences and provide them with the assistance and support they need to overcome obstacles.

- **Promote independence and autonomy:** In addition to giving your child structure and support, it's critical to promote independence and autonomy in how they manage their recovery process. Give your child the freedom to choose within the established parameters and assist them in accepting accountability for their own welfare. Give them the tools they need to take an active part in their own recovery by encouraging them to speak up for their needs and preferences with their treatment team.

- **Set a good example for your child by modeling healthy limits and self-care:** It's crucial for parents and other caregivers to set a good example for their children.

Make time for the things that will feed and refill you, and prioritize your own physical, emotional, and mental well-being. Establish limits on your personal time, energy, and emotional resources, and be forthright and honest in communicating your demands. You can help your child understand the value of prioritizing their own well-being and creating boundaries that support their recovery path by modeling good boundaries and self-care.

- **Establish structure and routine:** Make a timetable and follow it as closely as you can, incorporating regular meal times, therapy sessions, self-care routines, and leisure activities. Motivate your youngster to take charge of their schedule and get involved in creating and arranging their daily activities.

- **Seek support and advice when necessary:** Don't be afraid to ask family therapists or mental health specialists for help and advice if you're having trouble establishing rules or creating structure in your family. A qualified expert can provide advice on how to manage family dynamics, set up appropriate boundaries, and encourage consistency in a way that will aid in your child's rehabilitation. Keep in mind that you don't have to go through this path alone and that asking for help is a show of strength.

- **Work along with the medical staff:** Establish clear boundaries and give structure that supports your child's recovery goals by working cooperatively with the therapists, nutritionists, and medical professionals that make up your child's treatment team. To set limits about mealtime behaviors, treatment adherence, and other areas of your child's recovery journey, ask the treatment team for advice and input. Work together with the therapy team to create a well-thought-out plan to assist your child in healing, and be in regular, honest communication with them regarding your child's advancements and difficulties.

- **Put mealtime routines and rituals into place:** Creating regular mealtime routines and rituals might help your child recover from anorexia nervosa by offering structure and consistency. Establish regular meal and snack times and choose a peaceful, cozy, distraction-free area for dining. Encourage your child to help plan and prepare meals, and include special moments like sharing the day's highlights, setting the table together, and expressing thankfulness for the food. In addition to normalizing eating habits and fostering a happy digital age, these mealtime rituals and routines can help your child develop structure and balance in their life by setting boundaries for technology and screen time. Establish unambiguous rules around screen time, such as limiting the usage of gadgets right before bed and during meals. As you model good screen behaviors for your child, encourage them to participate in offline activities like reading, creative hobbies, or physical exercise. Establish specific times or areas in your home that are "tech-free" so that family members may interact and bond without being distracted by electronics.

- **Encourage self-care and relaxation:** Including self-care and relaxation techniques in your child's everyday routine can aid in the promotion of stress reduction, emotional control, and general wellbeing. Encourage your youngster to partake in relaxing and rejuvenating activities like yoga, meditation, deep breathing techniques, or outdoor time. Give your kids the chance to focus on self-care activities that feed their body, mind, and soul, and set an example of good self-care behavior by doing the same. You may assist your child in developing resilience and coping mechanisms that will aid in their rehabilitation process by encouraging self-care and relaxation.

- **Monitor and modify boundaries as necessary:** It's critical to monitor and modify boundaries as necessary to support your child's changing needs and objectives as they advance in their recovery. Remain aware of your child's development, difficulties, and feedback, and be prepared to review and adjust boundaries as needed. Supporting your child's healing process requires flexibility and adaptability, so be prepared to adjust rules and schedules as needed as your child's needs evolve.

- **Celebrate successes and progress:** No matter how tiny, acknowledge your child's accomplishments and progress in following rules and regulations. Celebrate small successes and accomplishments along the way, and give them credit for their hard work and accomplishments. Acknowledge your child's bravery and tenacity in overcoming the obstacles of anorexia nervosa recovery, and show your admiration and encouragement for their continued efforts. You may reinforce positive behaviors and motivate your child to keep going on their recovery journey by acknowledging and praising their accomplishments.

The Importance of Fostering Resilience and Coping Skills within Setting Boundaries and Providing Structure to Support Recovery from Anorexia Nervosa

For those recovering from anorexia nervosa to successfully manage the obstacles and setbacks they may experience along the road to recovery, they must develop resilience and coping mechanisms. Setting boundaries as well as creating structure can serve as a foundation for teaching your child resilience and coping skills, which will enable them to handle stress, deal with triggers, and recover from setbacks.

-Promote resourcefulness and problem-solving: Assist your child in the development of problem-solving abilities by asking them to recognize difficulties or roadblocks they face and coming up with possible solutions together. Urge them to use their assets, networks of support, and strengths to overcome obstacles and come up with original solutions to issues that come up while they're on their recovery journey.

- Instruct your child in emotion regulation: Give them the skills and knowledge they need to control their feelings and handle stress in a healthy way. In order to assist children relax and soothe their bodies and minds during stressful or anxious moments, teach them relaxation techniques like progressive muscle relaxation, deep breathing, and visualization exercises. In order to foster emotional balance and enhance self-awareness, encourage them to engage in mindfulness practices.

- Encourage the development of adaptive coping mechanisms in your child: This will help them manage triggers and temptations to participate in disordered conduct. Encourage them to partake in self-soothing activities, such as listening to music, taking up a hobby, or hanging out with encouraging friends or family, in order to divert their attention from unfavorable thoughts or feelings. Urge them to use artistic, literary, or journaling mediums to communicate their emotions.

- Offer opportunities for learning and growth: Teach your kids to see obstacles as chances for learning and growth rather than as insurmountable hurdles. Encourage children to adopt a growth attitude by reinterpreting failures as opportunities for learning and emphasizing their accomplishments, no matter how modest. Remind them that failures are a normal part of the healing process and encourage them to attempt new things, take chances, and venture outside of their comfort zone.

- Set an example of optimism and resilience for your child: As a parent or caregiver, show your child how to be resilient and optimistic by being optimistic, persistent, and upbeat in the face of adversity. Tell tales of your own successes and failures, emphasizing the value of resiliency, tenacity, and self-belief in accomplishing objectives and overcoming hardship. You give your child a strong example to follow as they make their own recovery journey by being resilient and optimistic yourself.

By implementing these techniques for establishing limits and offering organization in your strategy for aiding in anorexia nervosa recovery, you can establish a caring and encouraging atmosphere that promotes recovery, development, and adaptability for both your child and your family. By integrating techniques to promote resilience and coping skills into the framework of establishing limits and offering structure, you can enable your child to successfully navigate the difficulties of anorexia nervosa recovery and develop the abilities and strengths required to succeed in every aspect of their life.

It is important to remember to prioritize open communication, compassion, and support when setting boundaries. You should also remember to appreciate every accomplishment toward resilience, growth, and well-being. Together with your child's medical team, which consists of registered dietitians, therapists, and doctors, develop a thorough recovery plan because recovery is a team effort. Learn as much as you can about eating disorders; the more you know, the more capable you will be to help your child.

Chapter 9

Coping with Challenges and Relapses

Life can be unpredictable, everybody experiences difficulties and relapses and occasionally they can appear insurmountable. Difficulties or impediments that prevent one from achieving a goal are called challenges. Relapses are brief episodes of relapse or difficulty that occur following gains. Relapses and challenges are unavoidable. They are an inevitable aspect of growth and learning. Overcoming them fosters resiliency, ingenuity, and a feeling of achievement.

The path to anorexia nervosa recovery will inevitably include learning to cope with obstacles and possible relapses. This chapter will include helpful tips and methods to guide parents and other caregivers through these trying times with empathy, fortitude, and efficient assistance.

- **Recognizing Signs of Struggle:** It's critical that parents and other adults who care for children remain alert in order to spot any indications of struggle or possible relapse. These symptoms could include dietary adjustments, social disengagement, mood swings, elevated anxiety, or negative self-talk expressed. Parents who are aware of these signs can help their child get through difficult times by stepping in early and offering assistance when needed.

- **Open Communication and Validation:** Provide a secure and accepting atmosphere where your kids may share their ideas and worries without worrying about being judged or criticized. Encourage open and sincere communication, and accept your child's feelings and experiences even if you don't always agree with them. Building trust and connection with your child can be achieved through actively and sympathetically listening to their challenges.

- **Putting Coping Strategies into Practice:** Develop and put into practice coping mechanisms with your child to assist them in efficiently handling stress, anxiety, and other triggers. These tactics could be journaling, mindfulness exercises, relaxation methods, artistic endeavors, or asking friends, family, or mental health specialists for support. Help your child find coping techniques that work for them and assist them in implementing these techniques into their everyday lives.

- **Seeking Professional Assistance:** Don't be afraid to contact therapists, counselors, or other mental health specialists with expertise in eating disorders if your child has serious difficulties or appears to be headed for a relapse. A qualified expert can help your child get through challenging times and stop their condition from becoming worse by providing direction, support, and evidence-based interventions. Together with the treatment team, create a thorough care plan that takes into account the particular requirements and difficulties that your kid faces.

- **Emphasizing Self-Compassion and Resilience:** As your child progresses through obstacles and disappointments on their road to recovery, help them to develop self-compassion and resilience. Remind them that they are not alone in their problems and that setbacks are a normal part of the healing process. Urge them to be kind and understanding with themselves, and to stop obsessing on perceived shortcomings or setbacks and instead concentrate on their successes and qualities.

- **Fostering a Supportive atmosphere:** Encourage healing, development, and resilience in your family by creating a supportive atmosphere at home. Prioritize mutual support and encouragement among family members and promote open communication, empathy, and understanding. Provide a positive example of resilience and healthy coping mechanisms for your child, and show them that you are always there to support them as they face obstacles on their road to recovery.

- **Celebrating Progress and Victories:** As your child makes their way through obstacles and disappointments on their road to recovery, acknowledge and celebrate their accomplishments, no matter how minor. Congratulate them on their achievements and efforts, and show your admiration and support for their tenacity and resolve. By acknowledging and applauding your child's accomplishments, you support positive behavior and motivate them to keep going in the direction of recovery.

- **Recognizing Vulnerabilities and Triggers:** Assist your child in recognizing any triggers or vulnerabilities that can lead to difficulties or relapses during their recovery process. These triggers may come from internal sources like perfectionism, low self-esteem, or negative self-talk, as well as external ones like stressful circumstances, social expectations, or schedule changes. Through comprehension of their triggers and vulnerabilities, your child can create proactive approaches to deal with these difficulties and avert future relapses.

- **Creating a Crisis Plan:** Create a crisis plan that details what to do in the event of a major struggle or relapse with your child's treatment team. This plan should contain contact details for emergency support agencies, instructions on how to get help right away, and crisis or acute symptom management techniques. To make sure the crisis plan continues to be applicable and useful in meeting your child's requirements, review and update it on a frequent basis.

- **Promoting Adaptability and Flexibility:** Stress the value of adaptability and flexibility in overcoming obstacles and failures during the healing process. Anorexia nervosa recovery is rarely a straight line, with potential ups and downs. Encourage your child to view obstacles as opportunities for growth and resilience, understanding that failures do not define their entire journey or value. Assist them in creating coping mechanisms that foster flexibility and the ability to solve problems under pressure.

- **Addressing Mental Health Concerns That Co-occur:** Be aware that co-occurring mental health issues, such as trauma, anxiety, or depression, may make it more difficult to recover from anorexia nervosa or cause relapses. Together with their treatment team, make sure your child receives thorough evaluation and treatment for any co-occurring mental health disorders. Address these problems in tandem with your child's eating disorder treatment. You can assist your child in their recovery process by attending to underlying mental health issues and promoting resilience in their general well-being.

- **Taking Part in Family Therapy or Support:** If your child is struggling with recovery, think about taking them to family therapy sessions or support groups. These can help them deal with setbacks and relapses. Family therapy can offer a secure and encouraging environment for candid dialogue, cooperative problem-solving, and addressing family factors that might hinder your child's healing. Making connections with other families facing comparable difficulties can also provide validation, understanding, and useful assistance for your child's recovery.

Managing obstacles and possible relapses is a crucial component of the anorexia nervosa recovery process. Through the application of pragmatic tactics like candid communication, the cultivation of coping mechanisms, obtaining expert assistance, and creating a nurturing atmosphere, parents and other caregivers can proficiently assist their children during challenging times and enable them to persist on their journey toward recovery and adaptability.

The Importance of Building a Strong Support Network

For those in recovery from anorexia nervosa and their families, building a strong support network is essential as they battle through obstacles and relapses. During trying times, a supporting network can offer emotional validation, useful help, and encouragement, giving the person receiving care and their carers tremendous strength and resilience. When building a support network, keep the following important factors in mind:

- Make an effort to establish relationships with loved ones who are sympathetic, understanding, and supportive of your child's healing process. In times of need, these people can provide company, emotional support, and useful help. Inspire open dialogue and cooperation among family members, and inform them about anorexia nervosa and the finest ways to aid in your child's recuperation.

- Make contact with online communities or peer support groups designed especially for people recovering from eating disorders as well as their families. These groups offer a secure and accepting environment for people to share stories, offer support to one another, and trade useful advice and materials. Interacting with people who are traveling a similar path can help to validate one another, lessen feelings of loneliness, and inspire and bring hope for recovery.

- Seek advice and support from mental health specialists who treat eating disorders, such as therapists, counselors, nutritionists, and physicians. These specialists can provide your child with continuing support, individualized treatment plans, and evidence-based interventions to help them overcome obstacles and relapses in their recovery process. Together with the treatment team, create a thorough support plan that takes into account the particular needs and difficulties that your kid is facing.

- Benefit from the support services and educational materials provided by respectable groups that raise awareness of eating disorders and work to prevent and treat them. These organizations frequently offer workshops, information, support groups, and hotlines to those with eating disorders as well as their families. Make connections with regional or national groups to gain access to important information, campaigns, and networks of support in the community.

- Help your child investigate self-help techniques and materials that can supplement their medical care and support system. Self-help books, online classes, mindfulness exercises, and journaling activities that foster self-awareness, self-care, and perseverance in the face of obstacles and setbacks are a few examples of this. Give your kids the freedom to actively participate in their own healing process and look for services that suit their interests and requirements.

Children recovering from anorexia nervosa and their families can access the emotional, practical, and informational support they need to navigate through challenges and relapses with resilience and hope by creating a strong support network that includes family, friends, peers, professionals, and community resources. To support your child's continued recovery, never forget to place a high value on open communication, empathy, and teamwork within your support system. You should also not hesitate to ask for help from organizations and professionals when necessary.

The Significance of Fostering Resilience Through Setbacks

In order to heal and progress over the long term from anorexia nervosa, resilience in the face of setbacks is a necessary component of the recovery process. The capacity to overcome hardship, adjust to change, and prosper in the face of difficulties is referred to resilience. Recovering anorexics can acquire the fortitude, adaptability, and tenacity required to overcome obstacles and keep going forward on their road to recovery by strengthening their resilience.

The following are crucial tactics for building resilience in the face of setbacks:

Reframing Setbacks as Learning Opportunities: Help your youngster to view setbacks as chances for learning instead of as a result of failure. Assist them in realizing that obstacles are a necessary and normal aspect of the healing process as well as a chance for development and self-discovery. Urge them to consider what they can learn from the setbacks such as how to better understand triggers, hone coping mechanisms, or build support systems, and then incorporate these realizations into their continuing recovery efforts.

Cultivating Self-Compassion: Help your child develop self-compassion by urging them to treat themselves with kindness and gentleness when facing challenges. Assist them in seeing that obstacles and setbacks are normal parts of the healing process and that they don't define or lessen one's value. Urge them to engage in self-compassionate self-talk and to show themselves the same consideration and empathy they would provide to a buddy going through a comparable situation.

Fostering Adaptive Coping Strategies: Assist your child in creating coping mechanisms that help them remain resilient in the face of adversity. These tactics could be seeking assistance from reliable people, practicing mindfulness, using relaxation techniques, or developing problem-solving abilities. Encourage your child to use their assets, networks of support, and areas of strength to successfully navigate through obstacles and failures. They should also be encouraged to be adaptable and willing to try new strategies when necessary.

Encouraging Growth Mindset: Encourage your youngster to have a growth mindset by stressing the idea that obstacles can present chances for development and education. Motivate kids to see setbacks as transient challenges that they can overcome with hard work, perseverance, and fortitude. Assist them in establishing attainable objectives and acknowledge every step they take toward their recovery as proof of their continued development and resiliency.

Modeling Resilience: Set an example for your child by being resilient in your own life and in how you deal with setbacks as a parent. Tell tales of your struggles and disappointments, and how you overcame them to become stronger and more resilient. Emphasize the value of resilience as a crucial component in overcoming adversity, and model for your child healthy coping mechanisms, self-compassion, and constructive problem-solving techniques.

Adolescents recovering from anorexia nervosa can acquire the inner strength, flexibility, and perseverance required to overcome obstacles and keep moving toward a long-lasting recovery by cultivating resilience through setbacks.

The Importance of Fostering Self-Compassion and Embracing Imperfection

Embracing imperfection and practicing self-compassion are crucial elements of healing and resilience in the anorexia nervosa recovery process. Your child will be more resilient and self-kind to themselves as they overcome obstacles if you support them in cultivating self-compassion and a self-acceptance perspective. Here are some ideas for cultivating self-compassion and accepting flaws:

- **Exercise Self-Compassion:** Urge your youngster to show them self the same compassion and consideration they would a close friend going through a similar ordeal. Remind them that it's acceptable to make errors, encounter obstacles, or feel uncomfortable feelings. Also, reassure them that despite their difficulties, they are deserving of love and acceptance.

- **Develop Mindfulness:** Help your child develop mindfulness exercises that support acceptance of the present moment, self-awareness, and presence. By practicing mindfulness, you can assist your child in cultivating an attitude of non-judgment toward their thoughts, feelings, and experiences. This will enable them to examine their inner experiences with compassion and curiosity.

- **Confront Perfectionism:** Help your youngster in confronting their unrealistic self-imposed expectations and perfectionistic inclinations. Remind them that progress is more important than perfection and that they should be proud of every accomplishment, no matter how tiny. Remind them that getting well is a journey, not a goal, and that obstacles can be chances for development.

- **Practice Self-Compassionate Self-Talk:** Encourage your child to replace self-critical or negative self-talk with affirmations and language that expresses compassion for themselves. Reframe self-defeating attitudes or beliefs with words of self-compassion, empathy, and support to assist them. Encourage them to talk to themselves in the same way that they would a comforting friend, giving them words of support and consolation when things are tough.

- **Embrace Vulnerability and Growth:** Teach your child to embrace vulnerability as a normal aspect of life and to understand that it does not lessen their value or fortitude. Assist them in seeing that vulnerability is a common place for growth and that accepting one's imperfections is necessary for resilience, honesty, and personal development.

- Set an Example of Self-Compassion: Set an example of self-acceptance and self-compassion in your own attitudes and actions as a parent or other caregiver. When you suffer difficulties or failures, treat yourself with compassion and empathy. You should also be honest about your feelings and experiences. Your ability to be self-compassionate sets a strong example for your child to follow on their own path to recovery and self-acceptance.

During their anorexia nervosa recovery path, you can support your child to foster resilience, self-acceptance, and emotional well-being by encouraging self-compassion and accepting imperfection in the context of overcoming obstacles and relapses. Instill in your child the values of kindness, understanding, and acceptance toward oneself as well as the knowledge that they are worthy of love and compassion despite any obstacles they may encounter in life.

Part IV

Supporting Your Child on the Path to Recovery

Chapter 10

Understanding The Treatment Process

Supporting recovery from anorexia nervosa requires navigating the therapy process. This chapter will discuss the different aspects of treatment, such as medical interventions, holistic approaches, and therapy modalities, to assist parents and caregivers better understand and support their child's healing process.

- **Comprehensive Assessment:** A multidisciplinary team of healthcare specialists usually conducts a comprehensive assessment before starting any treatment. This assessment could involve discussions regarding the patient's eating habits, medical history, and treatment objectives in addition to medical, nutritional, and psychological evaluations. The assessment's objective is to obtain data in order to guide the creation of a customized treatment plan that takes into account each patient's particular requirements and difficulties.

- **Medical Monitoring and Stabilization:** These two aspects of treatment are frequently given top priority for people with anorexia nervosa. This could entail routine physical examinations, vital sign monitoring, laboratory testing to evaluate nutritional status, and urgent medical attention for any health issues. The goal of medical stabilization is to treat the medical issues brought on by anorexia nervosa and return the patient's physical health to a safe and stable state.

- **Nutritional Rehabilitation:** Restoring and upholding a positive relationship with food is the focus of this essential component of anorexia nervosa treatment. This can entail creating a structured meal plan in collaboration with a qualified dietitian that is adapted to the patient's dietary requirements, preferences, and therapeutic objectives. In addition to teaching about portion sizes, scheduling, and balanced eating, nutritional counseling may also cover anxiety and fear management techniques pertaining to food.

- **Psychotherapy and Counseling:** These treatments focus on the psychological and emotional elements of anorexia nervosa and are essential to its management. Cognitive-behavioral therapy (CBT), dialectical behavior therapy (DBT), family-based treatment (FBT), and interpersonal therapy (IPT) are examples of evidence-based psychotherapies that are frequently used to help people address distorted thoughts and beliefs about food, body image, and self-worth, develop coping skills, and enhance relationships and communication.

- **Medication Management:** To address co-occurring mental health issues including depression, anxiety, or obsessive-compulsive disorder (OCD), medication may occasionally be administered as part of the anorexia nervosa treatment plan. Under the guidance of a psychiatrist, psychiatric drugs such as mood stabilizers, atypical antipsychotics, or selective serotonin reuptake inhibitors (SSRIs) may be administered to treat particular symptoms and enhance general health.

- **Holistic Treatment Approaches:** Holistic treatment approaches include complementary treatments like yoga, mindfulness meditation, art therapy, equine-assisted therapy, or massage therapy. They concentrate on treating the patient's physical, emotional, and spiritual well-being. These methods seek to build a person's sense of balance and connection while also fostering self-awareness, relaxation, and stress reduction.

- **Family engagement:** For adolescents and young adults especially, family engagement is essential to the anorexia nervosa treatment process. Parent empowerment as an active participant in their child's recovery is a key component of the extremely effective treatment modality known as family-based treatment (FBT), sometimes referred to as the Maudsley approach. The goals of FBT are to improve family connections and communication, help the child regain his or her weight, and normalize eating habits.

- **Continuum of Care:** Overcoming anorexia nervosa frequently necessitates a protracted period of time and constant supervision. A continuum of care should be a part of the treatment process, catering to the patient's evolving requirements and obstacles as they arise. As the person advances in their recovery, this may entail switching from intensive treatment programs like inpatient or residential care to maintenance therapy, support groups, or outpatient therapy.

- **Collaboration with the Treatment Team:** A multidisciplinary team of medical specialists, the individual receiving treatment for anorexia nervosa, and the individual's family must work together to effectively treat the condition. Throughout the course of treatment, parents and other caregivers are urged to be involved in treatment planning, attend therapy sessions, keep in regular contact with the treatment team, and speak up for their child's needs and preferences.

- **Individualized Treatment Plans:** Acknowledge the significance of creating customized treatment programs that take into account the particular requirements, preferences, and difficulties that every person with anorexia nervosa faces. The age, gender, cultural background, medical history, co-occurring mental health issues, degree of motivation, and willingness for change of the patient should all be taken into consideration while designing a treatment plan. Work together with the treatment team to make sure that your child's unique strengths, objectives, and values are reflected in the treatment plan, and that their opinions and contributions are taken into consideration at every stage of the process.

- **Co-occurring disorders and dual diagnoses:** Recognize that co-occurring mental health issues or dual diagnoses could have an effect on how anorexia nervosa is treated. Post-traumatic stress disorder (PTSD), anxiety, obsessive-compulsive disorder (OCD), depression, and substance abuse disorders are among the co-occurring problems that anorexics may face. It is imperative to treat these co-occurring issues in tandem with eating disorder treatment in order to facilitate a thorough recovery and enhance general wellbeing.

- **Relapse Prevention Techniques:** Include relapse prevention techniques in the treatment plan to assist patients and their families in anticipating, recognizing, and skillfully handling possible relapses during the course of their recovery. Relapse prevention techniques can involve building a crisis plan to handle acute symptoms or crises, establishing continuous support networks, practicing frequent check-ins and follow-up sessions with the treatment team, and learning coping mechanisms to manage stressors and triggers. Relapse risk factors can be proactively addressed, and preventative measures can be put in place, to lessen the chance of relapse and preserve long-term recovery.

- **Gradual Exposure and Behavioral Challenges:** To assist patients in facing and overcoming anxieties about eating, weight gain, body image, and other facets of the illness, treatment programs for anorexia nervosa frequently include behavioral challenges and gradual exposure. Exposure-based treatments allow people to gradually reduce anxiety and develop adaptive coping abilities by exposing them to fearful stimuli or events in a safe and supportive atmosphere. Experimenting with flexible eating habits, questioning restrictive food-related ideas and regulations, and progressively adding previously banned items or food groups back into the diet are some examples of behavioral challenges. As a person advances in their recovery process, these strategies can support them in increasing their comfort levels, strengthening their resilience, and gaining confidence.

- **Extended Observation and Assistance:** Understand that recovering from anorexia nervosa is a protracted process that need for continued supervision and assistance after the initial stages of treatment. Over time, maintaining recovery, addressing remaining symptoms or obstacles, and preventing relapse may need ongoing care for individuals. Regular check-ins with the treatment team, involvement in support groups or aftercare programs, continuing dietary counseling, and access to resources and services that support long-term recovery and well-being are some examples of long-term monitoring and support. Setting long-term monitoring and support as a top priority helps people build a solid basis for resilient recovery and resiliency in the event of setbacks.

- **Celebrating Progress and Milestones:** To recognize an individual's accomplishments and encourage constructive behaviors, celebrate progress and milestones along the recovery journey. Celebrate every victory in the healing process, whether it's achieving a goal weight, finishing a treatment program, or learning a new coping mechanism. Acknowledge and commend your child for his or her efforts, bravery, and perseverance in overcoming obstacles and welcoming change. You should also show pride in and support for their continued dedication to becoming well. By recognizing and applauding your child's accomplishments, you encourage themto keep going forward on their path to health and wellbeing, validate their effort and commitment, and build their self-worth.

The Need of Attending to Underlying Psychological and Emotional Factors

In comprehending the anorexia nervosa treatment procedure. Recognizing and treating the underlying psychological and emotional issues that contribute to the onset and maintenance of the eating disorder is crucial, in addition to treating the physical symptoms of anorexia nervosa. Negative body image, low self-esteem, perfectionism, anxiety, depression, trauma, interpersonal challenges, and a need for control are a few examples of these variables. Treatment can enhance general wellbeing and encourage long-lasting recovery by addressing these underlying causes. In order to treat psychological and emotional problems, the key aspect is to:

Individual Counseling: Anorexics with anorexia nervosa can examine and process underlying feelings, ideas, and experiences that contribute to their eating problem in individual treatment. Evidence-based treatments that target particular symptoms and encourage psychological healing and resilience include dialectical behavior therapy (DBT), cognitive-behavioral therapy (CBT), and interpersonal therapy (IPT).

Body Image Interventions: These treatments aim to dispel the false assumptions and attitudes about one's own size, shape, and appearance that underlie the onset and maintenance of anorexia nervosa. For the purpose of fostering a more positive and accepting relationship with one's body, these interventions may include cognitive restructuring, exposure therapy, mirror exposure, and self-compassion exercises.

Emotion Regulation Skills: Training in emotion regulation skills enables people with anorexia nervosa to create flexible coping mechanisms for handling strong emotions and discomfort. These abilities can include the ability to identify and label emotions, identify and manage distress, identify and label emotions, and deal with difficult emotions and situations without turning to unhealthy coping strategies like disordered eating patterns.

Training Interpersonal Skills: To increase social support, fortify interpersonal bonds, and lessen feelings of loneliness and isolation, interpersonal skills training focuses on enhancing communication, assertiveness, and relationship skills. A network of support that encourages recovery and resilience can be established by those with anorexia nervosa through the development of good communication habits and the cultivation of supportive relationships.

Trauma-Informed Care: Treating underlying trauma-related symptoms and fostering recovery are crucial goals for those with a history of trauma or traumatic childhood events. To treat trauma-related symptoms and aid in anorexia nervosa recovery, treatment plans may incorporate trauma-informed therapies like somatic experience, trauma-focused cognitive-behavioral therapy (TF-CBT), and eye movement desensitization and reprocessing (EMDR).

When underlying psychological and emotional issues are addressed during the anorexia nervosa treatment process, patients can achieve complete healing and recovery that goes beyond symptom management to support resilience and general well-being. The efficacy of treatment can be increased by incorporating interventions that focus on body image, emotion control, interpersonal skills, and trauma healing. This will help individuals achieve long-term recovery and lead fulfilling lives outside of eating disorders.

Understanding Family-Based Treatment (FBT)

Family-Based Treatment (FBT), also referred to as the Maudsley Approach, is a highly effective treatment approach for adolescents and young adults with anorexia nervosa. Developed by physicians at the Maudsley Hospital in London, FBT is founded on the notion that parents and caregivers play a major role in assisting their child's recovery from an eating problem.

FBT is founded on several essential principles:

Family as the major Resource: FBT views the family as the major resource for assisting the child's recovery. Parents are empowered as active partners in their child's treatment, working jointly with the treatment team to assist recovery.

Externalization of the illness: FBT externalizes the eating disorder, distancing the illness from the individual's identity. This helps family helps family members understand the eating disorder as a separate thing that can be treated jointly, rather than attaching blame or guilt to the individual.

Normalization of Eating: FBT focuses on restoring the child's weight and normalizing eating behaviors as the major aims of treatment. Parents are responsible for managing and supporting their child's meals and snacks, ensuring consistent and enough nutrition to encourage physical and psychological rehabilitation.

Empowering Parents: FBT empowers parents to take responsibility of mealtime supervision and decision-making, offering them with the skills, knowledge, and confidence to assist their child's nutritional rehabilitation. Parents are advised to set clear expectations, develop mealtime routines, and handle reluctance or hurdles to eating in a caring and assertive manner.

Phase-Based Approach: FBT normally consists of three phases. In the initial phase, known as the refeeding phase, parents assume complete management of their child's eating to regain weight and stabilize medical and nutritional status. In the second phase, known as the transition period, parents progressively shift power back to the kid while continuing to provide support and direction. In the third phase, known as the maintenance phase, the focus changes to consolidating progress, treating underlying difficulties, and encouraging continued recovery.

Involvement of Siblings and Extended Family: Because eating disorders affect the entire family system, family members including other siblings may be included in the treatment process through family behavior therapy (FBT). In order to promote family cohesion and resilience, siblings may receive support and education to help them comprehend and manage their sibling's disease.

Cooperation with a Multidisciplinary Team: Family-focused behavior therapy (FBT) prioritizes treatment with parents at the center, but it also stresses working in tandem with a multidisciplinary team of medical practitioners, therapists, and nutritionists. Throughout the course of treatment, the treatment team offers parents and families direction, support, and knowledge, guaranteeing all-encompassing care for the patient.

Anorexic adolescents and young adults with FBT have demonstrated improved general functioning and quality of life, reduced symptoms of eating disorders, and promoted weight restoration. FBT is recommended as a first-line treatment for this population due to research showing its positive effects when compared to other treatment modalities. Families can benefit from FBT's family-centered approach to supporting anorexia nervosa recovery and promoting resilience and long-term wellness by empowering parents and caregivers as important change agents.

Parents and other caregivers can be extremely helpful in promoting their child's healing, resilience, and long-term recovery from anorexia nervosa by being aware of the treatment plan and actively involved in their child's recovery process. It's critical to address treatment with perseverance, empathy, and dedication, and to put your child's health and healing process first above everything else. Collaborating with the treatment team, encouraging your child's development, and acknowledging their milestones can help clear the way for a happier, healthier life after anorexia nervosa.

Chapter 11

Therapy and Counseling Approaches

Anorexia nervosa is mostly treated with therapy and counseling, which address the many psychological, emotional, and interpersonal components that contribute to the onset and maintenance of the eating disorder. This chapter will examine the many counseling modalities and therapeutic approaches that are used to treat anorexia nervosa, emphasizing their objectives, methods, and capacity to promote recovery.

- **Cognitive-Behavioral Therapy (CBT):** CBT is an extensively utilized, empirically supported treatment for anorexia nervosa that focuses on recognizing and addressing dysfunctional ideas, attitudes, and actions about food, weight, and body image. Through cognitive behavioral therapy (CBT), people can identify and confront false ideas and attitudes, learn coping mechanisms to control cravings and impulses to engage in disordered eating patterns, and create positive relationships with food and their bodies. In order to assist people in gradually and supportively facing their fears of certain meals or circumstances, CBT may also include exposure approaches.

- **Dialectical Behavior Therapy (DBT):** Originally designed to treat borderline personality disorder, DBT is a skills-based therapy that has been modified to treat eating disorders, such as anorexia nervosa. In order to control strong emotions, lessen impulsive behavior, and enhance relationships, DBT teaches people mindfulness, distress tolerance, emotion regulation, and interpersonal effectiveness skills. Instead of turning to disordered eating practices, DBT may assist people with anorexia nervosa in developing more adaptive coping mechanisms for handling stress and controlling emotions.

- **Interpersonal Psychotherapy (IPT):** IPT is a brief form of therapy that focuses on resolving relational patterns and interpersonal problems that support the development and upkeep of anorexia nervosa. IPT looks at how a person's eating habits and body image may be impacted by interpersonal issues, conflicts, and life transitions. IPT seeks to enhance relationships and aid in anorexia nervosa recovery by enhancing communication, resolving disagreements, and addressing interpersonal concerns.

- **Family-Based Treatment:** As covered in Chapter 10, family-based treatment, or FBT, is a nervosa treatment strategy that involves parents as active participants in their child's recovery. With the help and direction of a treatment team, family behavior therapy (FBT) gives parents the confidence to take control of mealtime supervision, weight restoration, and behavioral management. FBT tries to enhance family functioning and encourage long-lasting recovery by addressing family dynamics, enhancing communication, and giving parents the tools they need to support their child's rehabilitation.

- **Acceptance and Commitment Therapy (ACT):** ACT is a mindfulness-based therapy that aims to foster values-based behavior and increase psychological adaptability in the face of challenging ideas, emotions, and experiences. When it comes to eating disorders and body image

ACT can support people in accepting difficult feelings and thoughts while resolving to do recovery-oriented actions that are consistent with their beliefs. As essential elements of rehabilitation, ACT may help address experiencing avoidance and encourage self-compassion.

- **Group Therapy:** Those with anorexia nervosa can connect with others who are going through similar struggles in a supportive and affirming setting through group therapy. To address different parts of the eating problem, group therapy may concentrate on psychoeducation, skill-building, interpersonal processes, or experiential exercises. Peer support, constructive criticism, and social interaction are all possibilities that group therapy can provide, which can boost motivation and accountability during the healing process.

- **Nutritional counseling:** A crucial part of anorexia nervosa treatment, nutritional counseling helps patients regain and sustain a healthy relationship with food by educating, guiding, and supporting them in doing so. Personalized meal plans, nutritional deficiencies, food-related anxieties and beliefs, intuitive eating, and balanced nutrition are all areas in which registered dietitians collaborate with individuals. To help clients make realistic and long-lasting changes in their eating habits, nutritional counseling may also include meal planning, grocery shopping, culinary instruction, and meal support.

- **Mindfulness-Based Interventions:** When treating anorexia nervosa, mindfulness-based interventions including mindful eating, body scan activities, and mindfulness meditation may be used in addition to conventional therapies. Compassionate self-acceptance, nonjudgmental observation of thoughts and sensations, and present-moment awareness are all facilitated by mindfulness techniques. Through practicing mindfulness, people with anorexia nervosa can become more conscious of their bodies and hunger signals, become less reactive to situations involving food, and create a more compassionate and balanced connection with food and their bodies.

- **Expressive therapies:** Non-verbal and experiential means of exploring and expressing emotions, experiences, and identities are provided by expressive therapies such dance/movement therapy, theater therapy, music therapy, and art therapy. Through expressive therapies, people can gain deeper insights, process tough emotions, and express themselves in ways that might be difficult to do through spoken communication alone. In the context of treating anorexia nervosa, these approaches may encourage emotional healing, self-expression, and self-discovery.

- **Supportive Counseling and Psychoeducation:** Throughout the course of treatment, supportive counseling and psychoeducation give anorexics and their families knowledge, validation, and emotional support. These approaches could include educating others about the causes and symptoms of anorexia nervosa, talking about treatment alternatives and objectives, responding to worries and inquiries, and validating and empathizing with the difficulties and feelings encountered during the healing process. The goals of supportive counseling and psychoeducation are to provide people and families with the information, tools, and encouragement they need to navigate through the recovery process.

Body-Oriented Therapies

Somatic experience, dance/movement therapy, and yoga therapy are examples of body-oriented therapies that emphasize the mind-body link and the importance of movement and bodily sensations in the recovery process from anorexia nervosa. These treatments place a strong emphasis on reestablishing a connection with the body, raising bodily awareness, and letting go of trauma or tension that has been stored there. In order to encourage relaxation, embodiment, and self-regulation, body-oriented therapies may incorporate techniques like breathwork, gentle movement, body scanning, and guided visualization. Body-oriented therapies recognize the connection between the mind, body, and spirit and provide a holistic approach to recovery. The somatic components of anorexia nervosa are addressed, and holistic well-being is encouraged, by addressing the body's inherent intelligence and potential for self-regulation. Here are some additional considerations:

- **Somatic Experiencing (SE):** Developed by Dr. Peter Levine, SE is a body-oriented therapy that targets the physiological responses that the body stores in order to resolve symptoms associated to trauma and stress. By addressing underlying trauma or stressors that may contribute to disordered eating behaviors and by investigating sensations, movements, and bodily experiences connected with the eating disorder, individuals with anorexia nervosa may benefit from self-exploration (SE). The goals of SE are to support resilience, help the body finish its natural stress response cycle, and give it back its sense of safety and empowerment.

- **Dance/Movement Therapy:** This approach makes use of expressive arts, dance, and movement to help with body awareness self-expression, and emotional processing. Dance/movement therapy provides a nonverbal means for people to explore their relationship with their body, communicate feelings, and develop self-compassion in the context of treating anorexia nervosa. People can reconnect with their bodies, let go of tension, and grow a more positive and embodied sense of self via movement exploration, improvisation, and guided activities.

- Yoga Therapy: To enhance physical, mental, and emotional well-being, yoga therapy incorporates various yoga practices such as asanas (physical postures), pranayama (breathwork), meditation, and mindfulness. Yoga therapy provides a means for individuals to regain a connection with their bodies, foster self-awareness, and learn coping mechanisms for handling stress and emotions in the treatment of anorexia nervosa. Yoga may improve body acceptance, assist people control their nervous systems, and promote inner balance and tranquility. Yoga therapy sessions emphasize safety, gentle movement, and self-compassion, and are tailored to match the specific requirements and skills of individuals with anorexia nervosa.

- **Embodiment Practices:** These methods center on developing a stronger bond with the body and encouraging awareness and aliveness in the present moment. Progressive muscle relaxation, guided imagery, mindfulness-based body scans, and sensory awareness exercises are a few examples of these techniques. Through embodiment activities, anorexics can improve their ability to self-regulate and take care of themselves, become more resilient to stressors and triggers, and become more sensitive to their body's feelings.

- **Integration with Conventional Therapies:** By offering extra channels for inquiry, expression, and recovery, body-oriented therapies can enhance conventional therapies like CBT, DBT, and IPT. People with anorexia nervosa can obtain a more comprehensive and holistic support system that addresses the multidimensional character of their recovery journey by including body-oriented techniques into their therapy. Treatment teams and therapists can work together to customize interventions to each person's particular requirements and preferences, guaranteeing a customized and comprehensive approach to rehabilitation.

- **Mind-Body Connection:** The influence of physical experiences on emotional health and the mind-body connection are key concepts in body-oriented therapies. People can learn more about the relationship between their ideas, feelings, and physical experiences by developing an awareness of their body's sensations, actions, and postures. This increased consciousness can aid in the processing of emotions, improve self-control abilities, and encourage a feeling of empowerment and agency during the healing process.

By adding body-oriented treatments to anorexia nervosa treatment, patients can get access to more resources for recovery, self-awareness, and personal growth. On their path to recovery, these therapies give patients the chance to develop resilience and well-being, examine their inner experiences, and reestablish a connection with their bodies. In order to ensure a comprehensive and individualized approach to recovering from anorexia nervosa, therapists and treatment teams can collaborate with people to incorporate body-oriented techniques into their treatment programs.

We have looked at the many counseling techniques and therapeutic approaches that are employed to treat anorexia nervosa. The chapter covers a variety of interventions designed to address the intricate psychological, emotional, and relational aspects of the disorder, ranging from family-centered approaches like Family-Based Treatment (FBT) to evidence-based therapies like Dialectical Behavior Therapy (DBT) and Cognitive-Behavioral Therapy (CBT).

Chapter 12

Self-Care for Parents and caregiver: Maintaining Your Well-being

It is crucial for parents and other caregivers of kids and teenagers with anorexia to put their own health first in addition to aiding in their loved one's rehabilitation. This chapter explores the significance of self-care and provides tools and tactics to support you in overcoming the obstacles of providing care while preserving your own physical, mental, and emotional well-being.

- **Comprehending the Effects of Caregiving:** Be aware of the negative effects that providing care might have on your own health, such as elevated levels of stress, worry, and burnout. Recognize the psychological difficulties associated with seeing your child battle an eating disorder and the significance of taking care of your own needs in order to provide long-term support for your loved one's recovery.

- **Self-Compassion and Acceptance:** As you manage the highs and lows of providing care, cultivate self-compassion and acceptance. Be kind to yourself and accept that it's normal to experience feelings of overload, frustration, or uncertainty occasionally. Recognize that you're doing the best you can in a difficult situation and develop self-compassionate answers to your own problems and limitations.

- **Seeking Support:** Don't be afraid to ask your friends, family, support groups, or mental health specialists for help. Make connections with other parents and caregivers who can sympathize with you, validate your experience, and provide helpful guidance. To exchange experiences, resources, and coping mechanisms, think about joining local parent support networks, online forums, or support groups.

- **Upholding Healthy limits:** To safeguard your own wellbeing and aid in your loved one's recuperation, establish healthy limits with them if they have anorexia nervosa. Remain detached from enabling behaviors or power struggles and concentrate on showing love, support, and encouragement on a regular basis. In your relationships, promote openness, sincerity, and cooperation. If you need help navigating difficult circumstances, consult family therapists or medical professionals.

- **Managing tension and Emotions:** Learn coping mechanisms to deal with any tension, worry, or challenging emotions that could surface while you are providing care. To process feelings and relieve tension, try stress-reduction methods like progressive muscle relaxation, guided visualization, or journaling. To explore your feelings, obtain perspective, and create useful coping mechanisms for managing the difficulties of caregiving, think about attending counseling or therapy.

- **Practicing Self-Care:** Include activities that feed your body, mind, and soul into your daily routine as a means of prioritizing self-care. Engage in deep breathing techniques, mindfulness, or meditation to ease tension and encourage relaxation. Take part in enjoyable physical activities to relieve stress and improve your mood, including yoga, dance, or walking. Allocate time for interests, hobbies, and fulfilling pursuits, such as gardening, reading, and spending time in nature.

- **Making Self-Compassion a Priority:** As you manage the challenges of providing care, remember that you're doing the best you can with the tools and assistance at your disposal. Especially in times of self-doubt or difficulty, practice self-compassionate self-talk, affirmations, and acts of kindness toward yourself. Prioritize your own health as a crucial component of aiding your loved one's recovery from anorexia nervosa, and never forget that you too need kindness and support

- **Celebrating Progress and Achievements:** Give yourself credit for the growth, resiliency, and accomplishments you've made as a caretaker. Celebrate all of your little successes, life achievements, and development moments along the road, and allow yourself to feel proud of the difference you're making in your loved one's life. As a parent or caregiver, acknowledge and celebrate your unshakable love, devotion, and dedication, knowing that your support is crucial to your child's healing and well-being.

- **Educating Yourself:** Become proactive in learning about the causes, signs, and treatments of anorexia nervosa as well as the disease's recovery process. Participate in webinars, seminars, or workshops given by professionals in the field of eating disorders. To gain a deeper understanding of the condition and practical ideas for assisting your loved one's rehabilitation, read books, articles, and internet resources. You might feel more capable and prepared to face the difficulties of caring with assurance and clarity if you arm yourself with knowledge and information.

- **Putting Stress Reduction Techniques into Practice:** To assist you cope with the unavoidable pressures that come with providing care, incorporate stress reduction techniques into your everyday practice. To encourage relaxation and lessen tension in the body and mind, try deep breathing exercises, gradual muscle relaxation, or guided imagery. To develop present-moment awareness and stress-resilience, think about adding mindfulness exercises like yoga, tai chi, or meditation to your daily routine.

- **Building Supportive Relationships:** Make an effort to build relationships with friends, family, and other caregivers who are able to provide encouragement, understanding, and empathy. Tell people you trust about your experiences, struggles, and successes so they can offer you both practical and emotional support when you need it. As you prioritize your own well-being and face the challenges of caregiving, rely on your support system for perspective, company, and validation.

- **Seeking Professional Assistance:** Look for assistance from therapists, counselors, or support groups that focus on mental health, stress management, or caregiving. Take part in individual therapy sessions to explore your feelings, ideas, and coping mechanisms in a private, secure setting. Become a member of online forums or caregiver support groups to meet people who have gone through similar things and who can provide helpful advice, information, and encouragement. If your caregiving role is causing you considerable distress, exhaustion, or mental health issues, you might think about speaking with a healthcare expert.

- **Setting Realistic Expectations:** Recognize that providing care can occasionally be difficult and stressful, and set reasonable expectations for yourself as a caregiver.

Recognize that you might not know everything and that it's acceptable to ask for assistance, take breaks, and put your own needs first. Based on your unique constraints, available resources, and situation, modify your expectations and objectives; instead, concentrate on achieving small victories and constructive transformations over time. You may relieve unneeded pressure and give yourself the room to put balance and self-care first in your life by setting reasonable expectations.

- **Honoring Self-Care Achievements:** Give yourself credit for your efforts and accomplishments in self-care and placing your own health first as a caregiver. Acknowledge the significance of your self-care routines in maintaining your health, happiness, and resilience in the face of caregiving's obstacles. Take pleasure in your dedication to self-care and the benefits it brings to both your loved one's and your own wellbeing. As you progress on your self-care journey, acknowledge and recognize the importance of self-care as a necessary component of being a competent and kind caregiver.

You may sustainably support your loved one's recovery path while also promoting your own resilience, health, and happiness as a parent or caregiver by making self-care a priority. Recall that you are not traveling alone on this journey, and that being an effective and compassionate caregiver requires you to prioritize your own needs, reach out for assistance, and engage in self-compassion exercises.

Cultivating Mindful Communication

Understanding, connection, and support can be improved in your relationship with your kid or teen who has anorexia nervosa by implementing mindful communication techniques. To foster an atmosphere that is secure and encouraging for candid conversation and expression, engage in active listening, empathy, and nonjudgmental communication practices. Give your child security, support, and unconditional love while validating their emotions, thoughts, and experiences without passing judgment or offering criticism. You can help your kid or teen navigate their recovery path by building a sense of stability and acceptance, strengthening your relationship, and fostering trust via the development of mindful communication skills.

Investigating Creative Channels

For parents and other caregivers of children and teenagers suffering from anorexia nervosa, creating art can be a restorative and revitalizing endeavor. Creative expression, whether it takes the form of writing, painting, music, or gardening, provides an avenue for expressing feelings, digesting events, and discovering inspirational and consoling moments. Set aside time to pursue your hobbies and artistic interests as a way to express yourself and take care of yourself. Let go of judgment and expectations and embrace the creative process. Then, concentrate on the happiness and contentment that come from doing things that feed your spirit and spark your creativity. Despite the difficulties of caring for others, you can find new paths to resilience, self-discovery, and overall wellbeing by embracing your creativity.

Finding Joyful and Serene Moments

Finding and cherishing times of happiness, companionship, and relaxation is crucial while providing care for a child or adolescent with anorexia nervosa, despite the difficulties involved. Seek out opportunities to do things that make you happy, laugh, and fulfilled; they could include watching a funny movie, going for a leisurely walk in the outdoors, or engaging in a favorite pastime. In spite of the demands of caring, you may maintain your equilibrium and well-being, improve your mood, and refuel your energy reserves by making time for fun and relaxation. It's important to keep in mind that taking time out for happiness and joy is not only good for your own mental and emotional well-being but also provides a good example for your child or adolescent, showing them the value of happiness and self-care.

Part V

Finding Help and Resources

Chapter 13

Finding the Right Treatment Team- Professional Support Services for Families

Selecting the appropriate treatment team is essential for both individuals and families. Families may find it difficult to navigate the complicated world of anorexia nervosa treatment alternatives. In order to help the person with anorexia nervosa and their caretakers on their road to recovery, we will discuss the significance of putting together a thorough and encouraging treatment team.

Importance of Finding the Right Treatment Team

Specialized knowledge and skills are necessary to properly address the physical, nutritional, psychological, and relational elements of anorexia nervosa. With training and experience in treating eating disorders, medical doctors, registered dietitians, therapists, and psychiatric specialists are among the professionals with a variety of backgrounds and abilities that make up a multidisciplinary treatment team. These specialists can offer thorough evaluations, treatments based on scientific evidence, and individualized care catered to the particular requirements of those suffering with anorexia nervosa.

To effectively diagnose anorexia nervosa and analyze the disease's effects on physical health, nutritional status, and psychological well-being, a trained treatment team performs comprehensive examinations through thorough evaluations, the medical staff can pinpoint the root causes of the eating disorder's emergence and persistence and create specialized treatment programs that cater to each patient's unique requirements and obstacles. No two people with anorexia nervosa are precisely alike, thus tailored, specialized approaches that consider each person's particular skills, preferences, and circumstances are necessary for effective therapy.

Together, a collaborative therapy team creates individualized treatment plans that include evidence-based therapies and therapeutic modalities that are customized to the patient's goals and preferences. These plans address the patient's physical, nutritional, psychological, and relational needs. In order to guarantee coordinated care and communication throughout all facets of treatment, an integrated treatment team works closely together. Together, the member of the team can exchange information, organize treatment programs, and deal with any issues or problems that come up over the course of rehabilitation. This cooperative method encourages continuity of care, lowers the possibility of treatment fragmentation or gaps, and guarantees that patients receive all-encompassing, holistic assistance at every stage of their recovery process.

Anorexia nervosa also has a significant effect on caregivers and family members. In order to support families in navigating the difficulties of caregiving, comprehending the complexities of eating disorders, and developing efficient coping mechanisms and communication skills to aid in their loved one's recovery, a supportive treatment team understands the value of involving families in the treatment process.

A Comprehensive and Treatment Team for Both the Child with Anorexia and Their Caregivers

Professionals with a variety of backgrounds who specialize in medical, nutritional, psychiatric, and therapeutic therapies, as well as many facets of eating disorder therapy, often comprise a treatment team. In order to assess, diagnose, and treat anorexia nervosa, each member of the treatment team must take a distinct approach that addresses the disorder's psychological as well as physical components.

- **Medical Professionals:** Physicians, pediatricians, and psychiatrists are among the medical professionals who are essential in evaluating and keeping an eye on the physical well-being and potential medical consequences linked to anorexia nervosa. In order to handle any medical difficulties or co-occurring conditions, they coordinate medical care, provide pharmaceutical regimens, do medical exams, and keep an eye on vital signs.

- **Registered Dietitians:** These professionals focus on offering dietary guidance and assistance to people struggling with eating disorders, such as anorexia nervosa. In addition to creating customized meal plans and assessing nutritional needs, they also offer advice and instruction on intuitive eating, meal planning, and balanced nutrition. In order to treat food-related anxieties, difficulties, and habits, registered dietitians collaborate with people and their families. They also encourage a sustainable and healthful eating pattern.

- **Therapists and Counselors:** To address the psychological, emotional, and relational elements of anorexia nervosa, therapists and counselors such as psychologists, certified clinical social workers, and marital and family therapists—offer individual, group, and family therapy. They offer research-proven therapies like Family-Based Treatment (FBT), Dialectical Behavior Therapy (DBT), and Cognitive-Behavioral Therapy (CBT), along with other specialized modalities, to assist people in overcoming trauma or emotional problems, developing coping mechanisms, and challenging unhelpful beliefs and behaviors.

- **Psychiatric Services:** If a person with anorexia nervosa needs medication management for co-occurring mental health illnesses such depression, anxiety, or obsessive-compulsive disorder, they may need to see a psychiatrist. In order to provide comprehensive and integrated therapy, psychiatrists evaluate mental symptoms, prescribe and oversee psychotropic drugs, and collaborate with other members of the treatment team.

- **Eating Disorder experts:** Those with anorexia nervosa and their families can benefit from the specific knowledge and resources provided by eating disorder experts, which include physicians and treatment facilities that specialize in treating eating disorders. They offer thorough evaluations, research-backed therapies, and specialized support services catered to the particular requirements of people struggling with eating disorders. Depending on the severity of the eating disorder and the specific treatment goals, eating disorder experts may offer residential, intensive outpatient, partial hospitalization, or outpatient treatment programs.

- **Support Groups and Peer Networks:** For people with anorexia nervosa and their families, support groups and peer networks offer vital connections and assistance. These groups provide a secure and encouraging space for people to trade information, talk about their experiences, and get support and affirmation from like-minded people. Support groups can be offered in-person or online for greater accessibility, and they can be facilitated by peer mentors or trained facilitators.

- **Coordinated Care and Collaboration**: Members of the treatment team must work together to provide coordinated care in order to effectively treat anorexia nervosa. For integrated and comprehensive care that meets the various needs of patients with anorexia nervosa, medical experts, dietitians, therapists, and other specialists must collaborate and communicate with one another. Regular meetings of treatment teams are possible in order to plan treatments, review progress, and handle any issues or problems that may come up over the course of recovery.

- **Holistic Practitioners:** Some families may decide to include holistic practitioners on their treatment team in addition to conventional medical and therapeutic personnel. Acupuncturists, herbalists, and naturopathic physicians are examples of holistic practitioners who provide alternative methods for promoting mental and physical health. In order to address underlying imbalances and promote holistic healing, these practitioners may concentrate on complementary therapies like acupuncture, herbal medicine, dietary supplements, or mind-body techniques. Holistic approaches can provide additional skills and perspectives to help the entire well-being of patients with anorexia nervosa, but they should be strategically integrated and done so in partnership with other members of the treatment team.

- **Recovery Coaches and Mentors:** Throughout their road toward recovery, people with eating disorders and their families can receive personalized support and direction from recovery coaches and mentors. These experts could provide accountability, emotional support, and useful assistance to help people stay motivated, involved, and dedicated to their recovery objectives. In addition to having received specific training and competence in recovery-oriented practices, recovery coaches and mentors may draw from their own lived experience with eating disorders to offer individualized support and encouragement to individuals and families throughout the recovery journey.

- **Intensive Treatment Programs:** These may provide a greater degree of care and assistance for people with severe or complicated presentations of anorexia nervosa. Intensive treatment programs offer thorough and organized care in a therapeutic setting. Examples of these programs are day programs, residential treatment programs, and partial hospitalization programs (PHP). To meet the various requirements of people with anorexia nervosa, these programs provide a variety of therapeutic methods, such as individual therapy, group therapy, dietary counseling, and medical monitoring. If a patient has not improved enough with lesser levels of care, or if they need more extensive support than outpatient treatment can offer, intensive treatment programs may be advised.

- **Telehealth Services:** As telehealth services have grown in popularity, families can now receive specialist care and support from the convenience of their own homes. For those seeking treatment for anorexia nervosa, telehealth services which include online support groups, virtual therapy sessions and remote consultations with medical and nutritional professionals offer easy-to-access and convenient solutions. People who live in rural places, have limited access to specialized care, or prefer the ease and flexibility of virtual appointments may find telehealth services especially helpful.

- **Cultural Competency and Diversity:** To guarantee that patients and families receive care that is inclusive and sensitive to their cultural background, it is crucial to take these factors into account when choosing members of the treatment team. Look for experts who exhibit sensitivity, awareness, and respect for a range of cultural identities, experiences, and backgrounds. When selecting members of the treatment team, take into account variables including language, ethnicity, religion, sexual orientation, gender identity, and socioeconomic background to make sure that the care is appropriate, sensitive, and affirming of each patient's distinct cultural settings and identities.

- **Ongoing Education and Training:** To stay up to date on the most recent findings, recommended procedures, and developing trends in the field of treating eating disorders, members of the treatment team should place a high priority on ongoing education and training. Take advantage of conferences, professional development programs, and continuing education courses to increase your understanding and proficiency in working with anorexics. Treatment team members may deliver knowledgeable, evidence-based care that adapts to the changing needs of anorexic persons and their families by keeping up with developments in the field.

Families are able to obtain the information and skills required to effectively assist their loved one's recovery from anorexia nervosa by putting together a treatment team that is informed, understanding, and cooperative. In order to provide thorough, compassionate, and evidence-based therapy that addresses the physical, nutritional, psychological, and relational elements of eating disorders, each member of the treatment team is essential. Families, treatment providers, and those impacted by anorexia nervosa can collaborate to support long-term healing, wellbeing, and health.

Programs for Peer Support

Peer support groups provide a platform for individuals and families impacted by anorexia nervosa to engage with others who have also experienced the disorder firsthand. These programs give a safe and understanding environment for people to share stories, offer support, and get validation. They are led by qualified peer mentors or people who are in recovery. Peer support programs enable people to get assistance and direction from the comfort of their own homes. They can take the shape of online forums, in-person support groups, or virtual peer mentoring programs. Participating in peer support groups can provide individuals and families with invaluable perspectives, insights, and support from others who are aware of the particular struggles and achievements associated with living with anorexia nervosa. Peer support groups are a valuable adjunct to professional treatment, providing individuals and families undergoing recovery with an extra measure of community, empowerment, and connection.

Chapter 14

Educational and Non-Profit Organizations

Non-profit and educational organizations play a pivotal role in the landscape of activism, education, and support for people with anorexia nervosa and their families. This chapter delves into the vital contributions made by these groups, emphasizing their commitment to promoting hope, offering services, and increasing awareness among the community affected by eating disorders. For people coping with the difficulties of anorexia nervosa, these organizations provide a lifeline of support and empowerment through anything from helplines and support groups to educational programs and advocacy campaigns.

Come explore with me through the important work that these organizations do and the important role that they play in fostering awareness, healing, and connections for people with this difficult and complex eating disorder and their families.

- **National Eating Disorders Association (NEDA):** NEDA is a well-known nonprofit organization that supports people with eating disorders, such as anorexia nervosa, as well as their family. A variety of services are available through NEDA to assist individuals in need, such as support groups, instructional materials, online forums, helplines, and connections to other organizations. Through public education campaigns, policy initiatives, and community outreach programs, NEDA also promotes greater understanding of eating disorders, better access to treatment, and a reduction in the stigma associated with them.

- **Academy for Eating Disorders (AED):** A group of experts devoted to furthering clinical practice, education, and research in the area of eating disorders. In order to work together on cutting edge research, create best practices, and provide the eating disorders community with evidence-based information and tools, AED brings together researchers, clinicians, educators, and advocates. To foster professional growth and knowledge sharing among experts in the field of eating disorders, AED organizes conferences, workshops, and webinars.

- **Families Encouraged and Helping with Eating Disorder Treatment (F.E.A.S.T.):** An international group called F.E.A.S.T. works to support families who have members with eating disorders, such as anorexia nervosa. F.E.A.S.T. provides peer support networks, online forums, and instructional materials to enable families to connect, get knowledge, and overcome the obstacles of providing care while assisting their loved one's healing process. In addition to promoting empowerment, cooperation, and communication within the eating disorders community, F.E.A.S.T. pushes for family-centered approaches to eating disorder treatment.

- **The Alliance for Eating Disorders Awareness:** This non-profit group is committed to helping people and families impacted by eating disorders by offering outreach, education, and support. In order to encourage early intervention and access to treatment for eating disorders, the Alliance provides educational programs, support groups, and community activities. In order to address the prevalence of eating disorders and its effects on people as individuals, families, and communities, the Alliance also pushes for more financing, research, and legislative efforts.

- **Project HEAL:** Project HEAL is a nonprofit organization whose goal is to give people with eating disorders who are financially disadvantaged access to treatment and support. In order to assist people and families in overcoming obstacles to care, Project HEAL provides funding for treatment scholarships, assistance with treatment-related costs, and access to resources and support networks. In addition, Project HEAL supports campaigns for advocacy, education, and awareness to address the root causes of eating disorders and how they arise and persist.

- **Eating Disorders Coalition (EDC):** A non-profit whose mission is to promote federal funding, research, and policy efforts aimed at addressing eating disorders as a public health priority. In order to support legislative action, policy changes, and public education initiatives aimed at enhancing treatment access, lowering stigma, and promoting preventive and early intervention measures for eating disorders, EDC brings together individuals, families, professionals, and organizations. EDC advances measures that address the needs of people and families impacted by eating disorders by collaborating with legislators, government agencies, and advocacy partners.

- **Butterfly Foundation (Australia):** Based in Australia, the Butterfly Foundation is a nationwide organization that supports people with eating disorders, such as anorexia nervosa, as well as their family. The Butterfly Foundation provides information, support, and hope to people affected by eating disorders through helplines, online support groups, educational materials, and advocacy campaigns. Through community participation, public education campaigns, and legislative advocacy initiatives, The Butterfly Foundation also seeks to reduce stigma, increase early intervention and access to treatment for eating disorders, and raise awareness of the issue.

- **Center for Discovery:** For those with anorexia nervosa and other eating disorders, Center for Discovery is a top supplier of specialist eating disorder treatment programs. These programs include residential, partial hospitalization, and intense outpatient options. The Center for Discovery provides individualized treatment programs that are customized to meet the specific needs of each patient, as well as evidence-based therapy methods and interdisciplinary care teams. The Center for Discovery, which has facilities across the country, offers thorough, kind, and all-encompassing care to assist people as they work toward their anorexia nervosa recovery.

- **The Emily Program:** For those with anorexia nervosa and other eating disorders, The Emily Program provides individualized care in a comprehensive eating disorder treatment program. The Emily Program offers a continuum of care, including outpatient, intense outpatient, partial hospitalization, and residential treatment options. It has locations in several states in the US. The program provides evidence-based therapy modalities that are customized to each individual's specific requirements, including Family-Based therapy (FBT), Dialectical Behavior Therapy (DBT), and Cognitive-Behavioral Therapy (CBT). The Emily Program provides thorough, compassionate, and tailored care to assist long-lasting recovery. It also offers specific courses for people with co-occurring mental health issues, trauma histories, or other complex needs.

- **Eating Disorder Hope:** Dedicated to helping people and families impacted by eating disorders, especially anorexia nervosa, Eating Disorder Hope is an online resource that offers knowledge, inspiration, and support. A plethora of informative articles, blog entries, podcasts, and videos about recovery techniques, treatment alternatives, self-care advice, and inspirational personal narratives are available on Eating Disorder Hope. A directory of treatment facilities, support groups, and other resources is also available on the website to aid people and families in finding the care and support they require to deal with the difficulties of anorexia nervosa recovery.

- **Academy for Eating Disorders (AED):** The AED provides information and assistance to people and families impacted by eating disorders, such as anorexia nervosa, in addition to its professional membership.

AED offers seminars, online resources, and educational materials on a variety of subjects, including diagnosing eating disorders, locating treatment, and promoting recovery. In order to advance the field of eating disorder treatment and research, AED also organizes an annual conference that brings together patients, families, doctors, researchers, and activists.

- **Nourishing Success:** Using a holistic approach that emphasizes nourishing the mind, body, and soul, Nourishing Success is a program created to assist people and families on their road to recovery from anorexia nervosa. In order to support healing, resilience, and empowerment, the program combines nutritional counseling, mindfulness exercises, and artistic expression with evidence-based therapeutic techniques. For those battling anorexia nervosa, Nourishing Success provides information, motivation, and support through workshops, retreats, and online resources.

- **Beat (United Kingdom):** As the top eating disorder charity in the UK, Beat offers advocacy, information, and support to those with eating disorders, particularly anorexia nervosa. Beat provides training programs for schools, colleges, and workplaces to promote early intervention and raise awareness. It also offers helplines, online support groups, and resources for people, families, and professionals. Through public education and advocacy initiatives, Beat also pushes for more treatment accessibility, enhanced training for medical professionals, and a decrease in the stigma associated with eating disorders.

- **Anorexia Nervosa and Related Disorders National Association (ANAD):** A non-profit group called ANAD is committed to helping those who are impacted by anorexia nervosa and other eating disorders by offering support, advocacy, and education. In addition to educational programs and awareness campaigns, ANAD provides resources, support groups, and hotlines for individuals, families, and professionals. These efforts aim to decrease stigma, increase access to treatment for eating disorders, and encourage early intervention. In order to address the effects of eating disorders on people as individuals, families, and communities, ANAD also promotes financing for research, legislative changes, and public education campaigns.

- **Body Brave:** Located in Ontario, Canada, Body Brave is a non-profit organization committed to helping those with eating disorders, such as anorexia nervosa, by educating, advocating, and offering support. Body Brave provides workshops, peer support groups, and educational materials to enable people to question diet culture, develop body acceptance, and foster resilience during their road toward recovery. In order to address the root causes of eating disorders in Canadian society and their ongoing prevalence, Body Brave also promotes better access to treatment, mental health services, and community resources.

- **Organizations Dedicated to Eating Disorder Research:** The National Institutes of Health (NIH), the Eating Disorders Research Society (EDRS), and the National Eating Disorders Collaboration (NEDC) are just a few of the organizations that work to advance our understanding of and ability to treat anorexia nervosa. To improve outcomes for those with anorexia nervosa, these groups support research projects, share study findings, and encourage cooperation between researchers, doctors, and activists. Individuals and families can help the group working to create more potent anorexia nervosa prevention, intervention, and treatment options by funding research activities.

- **Online Communities and Support Groups:** These online spaces provide a forum for people with anorexia nervosa and their family to interact, exchange stories, and provide encouragement and support to one another. People can ask questions, seek advice, and find support from others who understand their challenges in a safe and supportive environment by visiting websites, forums, and social media groups devoted to eating disorder recovery. These virtual support groups can serve as a valuable adjunct to medical care by offering continuous encouragement, camaraderie, and affirmation during the process of healing.

- **Government Agencies and Health Organizations:** As public health concerns, eating disorders are addressed in part by government agencies and health organizations like the Substance Abuse and Mental Health Services Administration (SAMHSA), the World

Health Organization (WHO), and the Centers for Disease Control and Prevention (CDC). These organizations support prevention, early intervention, and treatment access for eating disorders, including anorexia nervosa, by disseminating knowledge, tools, and guidelines to medical professionals, legislators, and the general public. Individuals and families can remain up to date on the most recent suggestions and endeavors targeted at tackling eating disorders on a national and international level by obtaining information and resources from government offices and health groups.

These organizations are just a handful of the numerous nonprofit and educational groups that work to promote anorexia nervosa awareness, support, and advocacy for sufferers and their families worldwide. Individuals and families can discover empowerment, optimism, and connection through these organizations' services, knowledge, and support as they work toward anorexia nervosa recovery.

Chapter 15

Nourishing Hope Together: A Journey of Recovery

Every step forward in the anorexia nervosa recovery process is evidence of resiliency, bravery, and hope. This chapter honors the shared experiences of people and families navigating the difficulties, victories, and changes associated with anorexia nervosa recovery. It's a path filled with bravery in the face of adversity, tenacity in the face of setbacks, and fortitude in accepting change and recovery.

These people who have walked the journey of anorexia nervosa recovery and will share their stories of tenacity and endurance inside the pages of this chapter. These narratives offer hope, support, and unity to individuals who might be experiencing difficulties by showcasing the varied experiences, viewpoints, and insights of others who have set out on this path.

Through the prism of these stories, you will be able to see the evolution and healing potential of compassion, connection, and support. In fostering hope and resilience in the midst of the darkness of the eating disorder, we witness the impact of love, understanding, and acceptance. As they recover their lives, voices, and futures from the clutches of anorexia nervosa, we see the incredible bravery and tenacity of individuals and families. Also, make the experiences of others what you have in common, the awareness that you are not alone, and the prospect of healing and rejuvenation provide you comfort and strength as you set out on this path of introspection and discovery. I hope this chapter will be a lighthouse, guiding you through the difficulties and unknowns of healing and showing you the way to a happier, healthier, and more optimistic future. As you face the challenges of recovery, you can find comfort, healing, and a new sense of purpose by accepting the lessons acquired from personal experiences, developing self-compassion, and finding strength in supportive relationships.

By working together, we nourish hope, build resilience, and move forward with a future free from the stigma associated with anorexia nervosa. We find hope, healing, and completeness together on this journey of recovery.

Success Stories in Anorexia Recovery Embody Resilience and Renewal

Narratives of success in overcoming anorexia nervosa are potent symbols of the human spirit's resiliency and the potential for healing and rejuvenation. Here are a handful of these tales

Emma's Road to Recovery

I am really appreciative that I am writing from a position of healing since I never thought I would be. I went through a very terrible period in my adolescence, and I used eating as a coping method. I was searching for confirmation that I was deserving of life from someone or something, and for a little while, my eating disorder did. I felt like I accomplished something, and the more time I spent without eating, the more joyful I felt.

The depression lifted in that instant of achievement. Things quickly got out of control, and nothing seemed safe to eat. I felt I was winning the game for a time, but my eating issue kept taking control. It is a "more" sickness where there is never enough. I used to tell myself that everything would be alright once I reached a particular weight, but when I did, I didn't feel any better, so I just set a lower goal for myself, which was to be empty.

I needed my stomach to reflect my emotions, so I made an effort to look as broken on the inside as I felt. Even though I knew I was headed straight for death, I didn't care because my desire was to pass away. I used to think that it would be easier for my family if I died from my eating condition.

At last, I sought assistance and enrolled in a treatment program. Please remember that there is hope for healing if you can learn anything from my experience. I used to roll my eyes at people who told me that because I believed that recovery was something that only applied to other people. To be honest, I believed that rule to be applicable to a lot of things. I believed that, whereas everyone else needs food to thrive, I could live off of the air. I felt that while everyone else was deserving of assistance, I wasn't. Since then, I can assure you that I have come to realize that no human being is more valuable than any other. Neither you nor I can live off the air alone, but food is necessary for our survival, and human survival depends on one another.

Whatever the nature of the conflict could be, we cannot fight it alone, and it does get better, although it takes time. You will become stronger, and you will resurrect your life over the course of several months and years. I won't sugarcoat it; it was difficult, but I had to make the decision to value life over my illness. I still have to make that decision some days, but trust me when I say that it's worthwhile. My life now is something I never thought was feasible. I had denied that there was a future, but now I do.

I am constantly reminded that I can accomplish anything in my recovery with every new chapter in my life. Speak up if you require assistance, and continue battling. I assure you, it will be worthwhile

Melissa's Story of How She Reclaimed Her Life

The colors were the first thing I noticed. I was being forced to drink in the presence of the world, which had been a dull hallucination of my affinity for the dark and misunderstood for so long, which I did because that was all I had left at that moment. I drove to school confused and wasn't concerned or considering a recovery of any kind.

After three years of believing I viewed the world more clearly than ever, two days of constant carbohydrate consumption completely altered my viewpoint. The everlasting blue sky, the verdant foliage, and the splotches of CSUF orange on the students walking by. Springtime and all its sincerity. I was forced to face the reality that life was all around me as the noise of cars' engines energized me. It had never come to an end. I was thrilled after illegally parking my car and stuffing another fistful of almonds down my neck. I threw open my arms to the warm air and charged towards college with more enthusiasm than I have in years.

Being a little early for class, I made the decision to people-watch, force another very limited snack and sit on a bench. I found the students to be interesting; it was as though I had never seen them before. They were living their colorful, complex lives aloud and in the open. They were planning their weekend plans while eating, laughing, and yelling. Meanwhile, I was eating a browning apple with great fervor while perched on a seat. I started to realize how "other" I was. Even though I had known all along, I didn't feel any different this time. It dawned on me that I wasn't always that alienated from the world. I never imagined that I would have to try to understand it again, but all of a sudden, I was ready to give it a shot.

In the quiet of my bedroom, I confessed to myself for the first time that I was anorexic. Over the preceding few years, my mother and

Other worried parties had approached me numerous times about the matter, but I had always shrugged it off.

Naturally, I wasn't anorexic, because how would I have the stamina to work out for five hours every day if I were? My meals were extremely limited, yet even so, having three a day seemed like validation that everything was just fine with me. I had no idea that I had anorexia and a debilitating addiction to exercise or that eating disorders came in so many various forms and sizes.

It's a nightly habit for me to help sate my appetite by reading through food Instagrams, but I came across a profile that drew my attention. It was jam-packed with images of unconventional meals that resembled my regular fare dangerously close, not quite up to the standard of a seasoned food blogger. Upon deeper inspection of the bio and captions, I understood that this person fit the profile of someone recovering from anorexia. She had a kind of food journal where she could express herself and be honest with herself.

In search of knowledge, I combed through her captions. I found that practically everything she said resonated with me, it almost felt like something I had written. But it took me six more months of abusing myself before I was forced to visit an urgent care center due to severe heart palpitations, which made me realize that I couldn't continue this way for the rest of my life.

Since I came from a family with a history of vices, I've always associated the term "recovery" with drug or alcohol abuse. I reasoned that by keeping a strict schedule and working full-time, I had done everything in my power to save myself from that fate. I was an undergraduate senior, just about to graduate. I didn't make any blunders or run into any problems. I was a kid of light, exempt from the bonds of mortality.

Upon realizing my dire need for rehabilitation, I was immediately overcome with a deep sense of humiliation. I spent the bulk of my life striving for perfection as I'm unvarnished and nasty. I had no idea how to deal with eating disorders because I had never heard of someone recovering from it.

I knew exactly how common relapse was based on what the internet community said. I decided to disclose my eating issue to the public because I was desperate to get healthy and didn't think I could trust myself. Everybody approaches healing in a unique way so I decided to handle it alone. I was aware of my own stubbornness and understood that seeking treatment in a hospital would only lead to a relapse.

I saw that I couldn't completely rely on myself to make the best choices for my rehabilitation, so I made a compromise by scheduling therapy sessions. I also decided to share my hardships with the world in an irreversible way. Although I was ashamed of being so open to criticism, I was also afraid of who I was and knew that if I ever started to falter, people would hold me responsible.

I was mistaken in both cases. Within the first

minute of uploading the pictures, any discomfort I was experiencing vanished, and the comments began to pour in. People from all walks of life from acquaintances to family to strangers were encouraging me and praising my boldness. I wouldn't only be held accountable after that, I would continually be struck by how strong I am, overwhelmed by the abundance of love in my life and above all confided in by people who for the first time felt heard just as I had so many months earlier.

The hardest thing I've ever had to overcome was my recovery. It made me give in to my cravings. Individuals who take up eating disorders do so for reasons other than weight loss we want control. No, we require command. Above all, we must learn to live without need. Our goals are independence, prosperity, and power, and we think that the only way to achieve these is via restriction. The world won't ever be able to stop us, we already have that taken care of.

It was the greatest embarrassment to admit that I was hungry, especially considering how much my body was aching. My health was manipulated for a number of years, and it finally bit me. My body was desperate and clung to every ounce I gave it because it no longer trusted me. My period reappeared after a three-year absence. For a full year, every two to three weeks. At twelve years old, the hormones were raging even more intensely than they had the first time. It seemed like I was unable to maintain composure.

I had terrible memory. At best, my head seemed disorganized, at worst, it felt broken. My hunger was unbelievably voracious for several months at a time. Every day I felt sweating, exhausted, bewildered, worried, ashamed, and proud of myself. I was also thirsty, hungry, and scared. It was hard to concentrate on just one thing. I was unable to watch a touching scene on TV without crying.

My moods changed in a matter of minutes. For more than two years, these and other symptoms did not go away. Nothing was easy, but every day it was getting a little bit easier and that was the only thing that kept me going. I persisted because I thought it was too late to turn back.

I started pushing myself by going out to lunch and supper and putting my best face forward when I faced the menu. Along with coworkers, I gobbled up fatty meals and kept going back for more. I cooked enormous meals with my housemates, sharing the agony of the action with them was soothing and I felt like myself again. Eating developed into a social activity, a lovely custom and a universal tongue. I convinced myself that each bite of toast I put away was nourishing. I did this with six pieces at a time, since it couldn't get any worse, I reasoned that I might as well try my hardest.

According to research and my therapist at the time, the average recovery time is equal to the length of the suffering. I'm thinking back on my path as March 4, 2020, the third anniversary of my decision to heal, signifies my arrival at full recovery.

I had numerous desires to relapse but I never want to downplay that or the overall suffering involved in getting well. Most of the time, I felt like a whiny child, unable to communicate with the outside world. I had to start over socially. I had to retrain my skills as a lover, a friend, a sister, and a daughter. But now that I'm through the dark part, I can declare with confidence that every day, every weight, and every dread I endured were all worthwhile.

I'm dancing today as I heal. Growing up, it was always my favorite thing to do since it makes me feel beautiful, balanced, and free. I've returned, finally, after a long absence.

I laugh, I dance, and I eat. I came to New York to pursue my passion of becoming a writer something I had since I was a young child. I am enough, and life no longer feels like a continual pressure. I have the love of those that I've picked up along the road and my friends who have always supported me, I enjoy myself. How much I was missing out on was unknown to me.

My eating disorder has no clear origin or direct cause, hence it is impossible to identify one. But fear runs through all of the reasons. I was so confident in my abilities and so afraid that I would fall short in every aspect. I believed that I could remove the aspects of life that I found objectionable. I reasoned that if I hardened myself, it would be simpler to confront reality. However, it was my practice of transparency that allowed me the courage to actually save myself and improve my friendships with others.

There are moments when I long for the comfort my eating disorder gives me. I thought that being completely in control meant that I was unstoppable. I reasoned that it was my only chance of success. However, color makes life so much better. I doubt that my recovery is complete or perhaps I am, but

I'm by no means done learning. I'm not done loving myself more than I did yesterday, and I'm not done striving to improve myself as a person. One by one, I've vanquished my demons.

The Story of Cassie's Journey with Anorexia Nervosa

I never in my entire life imagined that I would be affected by anorexia nervosa. I still clearly recall stating, "I love food way too much that that would never happen to me," when I was younger. But it did occur, and anyone can experience it.

My battle with anorexia began when the initial lockdown was lifted. I was content with my appearance prior to confinement and had no concerns about it. But after the lockdown ended, I truly struggled and developed a sudden fear of social situations and people: would they think I'm attractive and intelligent enough?

Though it was on a different level, I have always overanalyzed everything. After graduating from high school, I embarked on a new journey by enrolling at a college where I knew only two individuals. When I started college, I promised myself that I would become "that girl," the one who went to the gym, only ate healthy foods, and put her appearance first—the kind of person you see on social media. I was just a different person when I first entered college. I was able to make friends, but I was prevented from being who I really was with them by this voice in my head that told me I wasn't good enough.

I was denying that anything was wrong because I wasn't "skinny" enough to have anorexia, even though my menstruation had stopped pretty suddenly. I realized there was a problem for the first time on our Easter family vacation. I love spending time with my family and am extremely close to them, but this time was different because I was worried.

I would have to eat "junk" or "convenient" food. That weekend, I seem to have screamed at my family several times, crying each time because they were taking me to a burger joint. My parents, unsure of what to do, began to express genuine concern and upset. However, I was still living in denial; I merely thought that I was attempting to maintain my health. I was unaware of the significance of the commotion, and now I see that my family was demonstrating their concern for me.

Things became worse after that holiday, and I was completely taken aback when I was praised by everyone for being "so productive" and "having my life together," which was ultimately what I wanted. My family is really important to me, and we have always been close, but I pushed them away when I was eating disordered. I remember crying uncontrollably once during therapy when discussing my sister. Although my sister and I have always been close, we just weren't able to communicate as much throughout my eating disorder because of the way she handles emotions. My sister and I went out for coffee and cake when I was still in recovery, and I remember crying in front of her and telling her I couldn't have cake and milky coffee. I recall my mother telling me that she had received a message from my sister stating that she was unable to handle the reality that there was nothing she could do to support me and could no longer be around me.

I stayed away from social gatherings where I knew there would be food. My anorexia overtook me, therefore I never felt as close to people since they didn't know who I was. My love for my family and friends was one of the main motivators for me to get well; life wouldn't be worth living without them. I believe there is a common misperception regarding anorexia that I never stopped eating or going out, but I could see that I wasn't the same person I used to be.

I realized I needed to start receiving anorexia treatment after I saw the doctor for the third time regarding my menstruation. The most terrifying part is that I was unaware that I had dropped a significant amount of weight since my last visit with the doctor. I never weighed myself while I had an eating disorder because I didn't want to be skinny I just wanted to be healthy and make my family proud of me for being what I considered to be perfect.

Fortunately, I was put on a program right away and received assistance right away. I am really appreciative that I received assistance at that time. It took me a while to realize anything was wrong, even after I'd made the initial step toward rehabilitation. It was not a simple or fast cure; I still avoided people and was preoccupied by my anorexia. I was able to share my tale with my weekly therapist, and as a result, I began to realize that perhaps I wasn't ok and that perhaps the "healthy" lifestyle I had imagined myself leading wasn't all that healthy.

I spent a long time denying that I needed to acquire weight, so at first I found it difficult to put on weight, but I was determined to move on with my life, so I concentrated on my academics and applying to universities.

Many people were afraid of me if I went to college even though I was told I wouldn't be able to go after the summer, I was adamant that I wouldn't let my life end. Honestly, attending university was the best decision I've ever made. My anorexia was not going to wreck another chapter of my life, so I realized I had to deal with it.

My councillor helped me a lot when I moved to a new place, and the nicest part was that, unlike at home, no one at university knew I was the anorexic girl. I therefore relied on my personality to advance and create acquaintances. I now understand that being an unrealistic imitation of what I once thought of as "perfection" is so, so much less essential than who I am as a person. Above everything, I should put myself first and make sure I'm nourishing myself to have the energy to be the best version of myself.

My loved ones genuinely don't care how I appear as long as I'm content; they just adore me for who I am. Now that I know that. I will never forget the sincere grins on the faces of everyone I knew when I finally called them to tell them I was getting out of treatment.

It took me a long time to get to this point, but I now know that I deserve to be happy and have learned to appreciate myself much more. I go out to eat on a whim and discover that the world has returned to its former splendor. In addition, my sister and my pals are back with me, and I no longer ignore them. Just by being myself over text, I've been able to build closer relationships with people, even some I never felt connected to before developing anorexia.

I am aware that anorexia does not go away quickly. We can all be affected by this protracted struggle, but we can prevail over it. Throughout my experience, I have come to realize one positive thing: I am a strong individual. We can accomplish anything we set our minds to, since we are all powerful individuals with extraordinary minds that we use for good.

One of the most difficult conditions to recover from is anorexia. There have been ups and downs, and at times I've wished I could just vanish, but I know that if I can overcome anorexia, I can overcome anything.

A Mother's Story of How They Seized Control

2018 presented its challenges to the global community. We witnessed some shocking political decisions made both domestically and internationally. Seeing 2018 go was a relief for many of us.

On a far more intimate level, our family first encountered our eating disorder in 2018. I refer to "our" eating disorder (ED) since, as a family of four, we have each had a unique relationship with our youngest daughter's ED.

She developed a preoccupation with eating

approximately six months ago, which is when our journey to the ED service began. At first, I assumed she was merely trying to eat healthier by avoiding "bad food" and sticking to a regular schedule of nutritious meals. But over the course of the following three to four months, she gradually made the transition from a good diet to more activity and, eventually, an environment where she was always talking about food. She put hours into crafting exquisite recipe sheets and typed out recipes for foods she didn't plan to eat. As her parents, we sensed that our happy, gregarious, witty, laid-back little girl was gradually giving way to a much more depressed, less energetic, solitary person who avoided social interactions.

She assured us that she was eating her school lunch, and we responded to her changing body size and shape with support when she ate supper with us that evening. We went to Pause for assistance, and she grudgingly talked to a staff member who reassured her that she wasn't the only one who felt self-conscious about the size and form of her body. She was assisted by an FTB body image group in gradually realizing the links between her body image and external pressures such as social media, celebrity culture, and body image.

Quite plainly, I would respond, "What do you wish you had known...?" that you didn't know in the early months of her ED. As a parent, trust your instincts. Nobody knows your child like you do. As soon as you sense that something is changing, seek assistance. I regret not having contacted her school sooner to see if she was eating her lunch or if her participation or behavior had altered. Our lovely daughter's physical and emotional well-being comes first, not because I believed her to be a liar.

I would also advise parents to take use of the abundance of incredibly helpful information and resources available online. When the time came, reading about recovery tales gave us parents hope and enabled her to understand that healing is a drawn-out, difficult, but valuable process.

As a family, we have benefited from the expertise, consideration, and support of the nurses, dieticians, psychologists, and family therapists. Most significantly, they have reaffirmed to us as a family and as parents that we are the experts in our own experience. They have also taken the time to listen to us as a unit and have helped each of us individually through the difficult times. No one else understands what it's like to raise her. to support her as she starts to reclaim control from the ED, little by little, with amazing tenacity and resolve. Although we have benefited from the experience and expertise of experts, I believe that, when I look back on 2018, our family has finally regained control, faced the ED head-on, and refused to allow it to destroy our little and priceless family.

We are grateful to the ED nurse, dietitian, clinical psychologist, and family therapy team for their support and assistance as we navigate the world of an emergency department.

These inspirational and uplifting tales of victory over anorexia nervosa serve as a constant reminder that healing is attainable and that no one has to travel this path alone. A future full of opportunity, happiness, and fulfillment is within reach for those suffering from anorexia nervosa, provided they have the fortitude, tenacity, and support of others.

Appendix: Resources and References

National Eating Disorders Association (NEDA): Website: www.nationaleatingdisorders.org
NEDA offers a wide range of resources, including helplines, online forums, educational materials, and support groups, for individuals and families affected by eating disorders, including anorexia nervosa.

Academy for Eating Disorders (AED): Website: www.aedweb.org
AED provides access to cutting-edge research, professional development opportunities, and evidence-based resources for professionals working in the field of eating disorders, including anorexia nervosa.

Families Empowered and Supporting Treatment of Eating Disorders (F.E.A.S.T.): Website: www.feast-ed.org
F.E.A.S.T. offers online forums, peer support networks, and educational resources for

families supporting a loved one with an eating disorder, including anorexia nervosa.

The Alliance for Eating Disorders Awareness:
Website: www.allianceforeatingdisorders.com
The Alliance offers support groups, educational programs, and advocacy initiatives to promote awareness, reduce stigma, and improve access to treatment for eating disorders, including anorexia nervosa.

Project HEAL: Website: www.theprojectheal.org
Project HEAL provides financial assistance for treatment scholarships, support for treatment-related expenses, and access to resources and support networks for individuals and families affected by eating disorders, including anorexia nervosa.

Eating Disorders Coalition (EDC): Website: www.eatingdisorderscoalition.org
EDC advocates for increased federal funding, research, and policy initiatives to address eating disorders as a public health priority, including anorexia nervosa.

Butterfly Foundation (Australia): Website: www.thebutterflyfoundation.org.au
The Butterfly Foundation offers helplines, online support groups, educational resources, and advocacy initiatives to support individuals and families affected by eating disorders, including anorexia nervosa, in Australia.

Center for Discovery: Website: www.centerfordiscovery.com
Center for Discovery offers specialized eating disorder treatment programs, including residential, partial hospitalization, and intensive outpatient programs, for individuals with anorexia nervosa and other eating disorders.

Beat (United Kingdom): Website: www.beateatingdisorders.org.uk
Beat provides support, information, and advocacy for individuals and families affected by eating disorders, including anorexia nervosa, in the United Kingdom.

Eating Disorders Resource Center (EDRC): Website: www.edrcsv.org
EDRC offers support groups, workshops, and educational events to promote awareness, provide information, and foster community connection for those impacted by eating disorders, including anorexia nervosa.

National Association of Anorexia Nervosa and Associated Disorders (ANAD): Website: www.anad.org
ANAD offers helplines, support groups, and resources for individuals and families affected by anorexia nervosa and other eating disorders. They also advocate for policy changes, research funding, and public education

initiatives to address the impact of eating disorders on individuals, families, and communities.

The Emily Program: Website: www.emilyprogram.com
The Emily Program provides comprehensive, evidence-based care for individuals with anorexia nervosa and other eating disorders. With a focus on holistic healing and personalized treatment plans, The Emily Program offers outpatient, intensive outpatient, partial hospitalization, and residential programs at locations across several states.

The Alliance for Eating Disorders Awareness (Canada): Website: www.allianceforEDA.ca
The Alliance for Eating Disorders Awareness is a Canadian non-profit organization dedicated to raising awareness, providing support, and advocating for individuals and families affected by eating disorders, including anorexia. They

offer educational programs, support groups, and community events to promote early intervention, reduce stigma, and improve access to treatment for eating disorders in Canada.

Body Brave: Website: www.bodybrave.ca
Body Brave is a non-profit organization based in Ontario, Canada, offering support, education, and advocacy for individuals affected by eating disorders, including anorexia nervosa. They provide peer support groups, workshops, and educational resources to empower individuals to challenge diet culture, build body acceptance, and cultivate resilience in their recovery journey.

Eating Disorder Hope: Website: www.eatingdisorderhope.com
Eating Disorder Hope is an online resource dedicated to providing information, support, and inspiration for individuals and families affected by eating disorders, including anorexia nervosa. They offer articles, blog posts,

recovery stories, and online forums to help individuals find hope and healing on their journey to recovery.

These resources provide valuable support, information, and guidance for individuals and families affected by anorexia nervosa. Whether seeking treatment options, educational materials, advocacy initiatives, or peer support, these organizations offer a lifeline of support for those navigating the challenges of recovery and empower individuals on their journey to recovery and healing.

ACKNOWLEDGEMENT

To everyone who contributed to the creation of "How To Parent A Child With Eating Disorder(anorexia): Understanding and Supporting Your Child's Recovery- A Complete Guide" my sincere gratitude is extended.

First and foremost, I would like to express my sincere gratitude to the people and families who shared their life experiences, insights, and tales with me. This book has been inspired by your bravery, resiliency, and willingness to share your emotions, and I am incredibly appreciative of your generosity and trust.

Additionally, I owe a debt of gratitude to the committed specialists and authorities in the field of eating disorders who offered priceless advice, know-how, and encouragement throughout the composition process. Your knowledge and commitment to serving others have really enhanced my book, and I am grateful that I was able to work with you.

Furthermore, I am grateful to the Freepik team for supplying the lovely photos included in the creation of the book cover. Your imaginative input has improved the book's aesthetic appeal and meaningfully brought its message to life.

I also want to express my gratitude to my friends, family, and colleagues for their continuous understanding, support, and encouragement along this journey. I am very grateful that you are in my life because your support, love, and faith in me have given me courage and inspiration every day.

Lastly, I would like to express my gratitude to all of the readers of the book. My goal is that the knowledge, perspectives, and resources offered within the pages of the book will help parents and caregivers, as well as the child affected by anorexia nervosa, by offering support, guidance, and hope. I also hope that they will foster a culture of compassion, understanding, and healing in our communities.

Jennifer M. Stevens

Made in the USA
Monee, IL
07 April 2025